*The Renaissance Imagination
Important Literary and Theatrical Texts
from the Late Middle Ages
through the Seventeenth Century*

Stephen Orgel
Editor

AN ENTERLUDE CALLED LUSTY IUUENTUS,
Liuely describyng the frailtie of youth: of nature, prone to vyce: by grace and good councell traynable to vertue

by R. Wever

An old-spelling critical edition

edited by
Helen Scarborough Thomas

The Renaissance Imagination
Volume 2

GARLAND PUBLISHING, INC.
NEW YORK & LONDON
1982

Copyright © 1982 by Helen Scarborough Thomas
All rights reserved

Library of Congress Cataloging in Publication Data

Wever R.
   An enterlude called Lusty Iuuentus.

   (The Renaissance imagination ; v. 2)
   Bibliography: p.
   I. Thomas, Helen Scarborough, 1917–
II. Title.   III. Title: Enterlude called Lusty
Juventus.   IV. Series.
PR3190.W3A7   1982   822'.2   80-9008
ISBN 0-8240-9406-9

Printed on acid-free, 250-year-life paper
Manufactured in the United States of America

*To my husband Joe David Thomas,
molder of my mind.*

CONTENTS

	page
Preface	ix
Introduction	
Texts and Author	xi
Dating in Relation to Theology:	
Henrician Theological Context	xiii
Edwardian Theological Context	xxviii
Dramatic and Literary Qualities	xxxix
Dramatic Context — Early Sixteenth Century	xlviii
Lusty Juventus, The Booke of Sir Thomas Moore, and Shakespeare	lviii
Notes on the Present Text	lxiv
Text	3
Textual Notes	55
Glosses	77
Bibliography	83

PREFACE

Lusty Juventus (sixteenth-century Anglo-Latin for Flaming Youth) is a rather badly neglected and certainly under-anthologized play, especially when we consider the good fortune in the marketplace of ideas of its Catholic equivalent, *Everyman,* dating from a generation or two earlier. Teachers wishing to use R(ichard?) Wever's moral interlude, about the ways of sin and redemption, in courses in Early English Drama are hampered by the lack of a scholar's critical edition and of a textbook suitable for student reading. Within these covers I have attempted to furnish both simultaneously, by providing a fully collated and carefully edited old spelling text of *Lusty Juventus.*

In my Introduction, I suggest and defend, without dogmatic insistence, a probable re-dating of the play to push it back from the Edwardian period to the last few years of Henry VIII's reign. Because of the nature of the evidence, the Introduction is organized mainly on a basis of the constantly shifting theological tides during the long Henrician era and the brief reign of his unfortunate son Edward VI. As the reader will soon see, such sweeping terms as "Catholic," "Protestant," "Puritan," and "Lutheran" are next to useless as clear indicators of what was actually happening in England between 1533 and the accession of "Bloody" Mary in 1553. A very fine reading, even a reading between the lines, of the documentation of those unsettled times is necessary.

I shall not attempt a roster of all the generous persons who have encouraged or assisted me in the extensive research reflected in this little volume. I must, however, mention the administration and the English Department of the University of Houston, who enabled me to go to the British Museum and the Bodleian; Professors John McNamara, William B. Hunter, Jr., and Niels C. Nielsen, Jr.; and my girl Friday, Bonnie Driggers.

H. S. T.

INTRODUCTION

Texts and Author

An Enterlude called Lusty Iuuentus. Liuely describing the frailtie of youth: of nature, prone to vyce: by grace and good councell traynable to vertue, by R. Wever, has survived in six copies from three separate sixteenth-century editions:
1. "Imprinted at London in Paules churche yeard, by Abraham Uele, at the sygne of the Lambe" (single copy extant, Bodleian Library, Oxford).
2. "Imprynted at London, in Lothbury, ouer agaynst Sainct Margarits Church, by Wyllyam Copland" (3 copies extant: British Library, Huntington Library, and Pforzheimer Library).
3. "Imprinted at London by Iohn Awdely dwelling in the litle Britayne strete without Aldersgate" (2 copies extant: British Library and Huntington Library).

The interlude was not published again until the eighteenth century when Thomas Hawkins included it in his collection, *The Origin of the English Drama, illustrated in its various species, viz. Mystery, Morality, Tragedy, and Comedy* . . . (Oxford: Clarendon, 1773). It was reprinted in the nineteenth century by W. Carew Hazlitt in *A Select Collection of Old English Plays* . . . (London: Reeves and Turner, 1874). In the twentieth century, John S. Farmer reprinted the play in *The Dramatic Writings of Richard Wever and Thomas Ingelend* (London: Early English Drama Society, 1905) and in a facsimile reprint of the newly discovered Awdely quarto in 1907. The most recent reproduction is the facsimile reprint of the Vele edition for the Malone Society, edited by J. M. Nosworthy, *Lusty Juventus* (Oxford: Univ. Press, 1971).[1] There is no previous critical edition of the interlude based on a collation of all three extant sixteenth-century editions.

Although the textual relationship of the three editions is not certain, Nosworthy argues convincingly for the Vele text as *editio princeps* and for a Vele-Copland-Awdely sequence, concluding that "the combined testimony of typography, spelling, and transmitted error argues that each of the subsequent editions was printed from its immediate predecessor" (pp. vii-xxi). In accord with Nosworthy's conclusions, this edition follows the Vele text as copy-text with some substituted readings from the Copland and Awdely texts and a comprehensive listing of substantive variants in all three editions.

Since none of the three editions is dated, evidence for their times of printing comes chiefly from the dates of the activities of the printers. Abraham Vele began printing in 1547 and turned his printing office over to William How in 1566;[2] so the date of his edition of *Lusty Juventus* would fall somewhere in that period, probably between 1547 and 1553 — during years of the reign of Edward VI when the final prayer for a king and council would not need altering to a prayer for the queen and her council as was done in the Copland and Awdely editions. Those two editions must date from the period of Queen Elizabeth, for it is improbable that Wever's play would have been printed in the reign of the Catholic Queen Mary. Since William Copland's printing from his shop in Lothbury dates from 1562 to his death in 1568, his edition can be placed within these limits. The dates for John Awdely's edition may be set somewhere between 1559 and his death in 1575, and if the assumption is right that Copland's is the intermediate edition between Vele's and Awdely's, the Awdely edition must be dated after 1562 when Copland first moved to the Lothbury address, and according to Nosworthy "presumably" after the death of Copland in 1568. More precise dating of these editions is not possible.

An entry in the Register of the Stationers' Company only complicates the problem of dating the three extant editions. Under the year 1560-1, John King is recorded as paying for a license for the printing of "a playe called *Juventus* . . ." but if he did print an edition of *Lusty Juventus,* no copy has survived. Nosworthy suggests that perhaps King's rights to publish the interlude were acquired from Vele, whose edition had appeared earlier without registration, and that the rights were then transferred to Copland, resulting in his edition sometime between 1562 and 1568.[3]

About the author of *Lusty Juventus* we know only that he was named R. Wever, whether Richard or Robert or otherwise, we do not know. There was a Richard Wever or Weyver, as Nosworthy points out, who was an Oxford student in 1524, perhaps a Fellow of St. Chad's College, Shrewsbury, in 1546, prebend of Bubbenhall in the Lichfield diocese from 1549 to 1554, and prebend of Hansacre until 1559.[4] Identifying this Wever with the author of *Lusty Juventus* is only conjecture, though it is certainly likely that the author of the interlude was a cleric. Nosworthy also notes that Foxe in his *Acts and Monuments* "names a Richard Wever as one of a large number of priests and laymen examined at Lichfield in September of 1556," but does not mention him further. "The resultant picture," writes Nosworthy, "if all these records relate to the same person, is of an Oxford theologian who operated peacefully in the Lichfield diocese under the tolerant sway of Bishop Sampson and whose troubles such as they were, began when Sampson's successor, Ralph Baynes, invoked the full rigours of the Marian persecution."[5]

Notes

[1] All future references to Nosworthy are to the Introduction in this reprint of *Lusty Juventus*.

[2] The information in this section about the printers is taken from Edward G. Duff, *A Century of the English Book Trade* [1457-1557] (London: for the Bibliographical Society, 1905), pp. 161-162, 32-33, and 5. Paul G. Morrison, *Index to Printers, Publishers and Booksellers in A.W. Pollard and G.R. Redgrave A Short-Title Catalogue . . .* (Charlottesville, Virginia: Bibliographical Society of Virginia, 1950), dates Vele's first printed book *(STC* 2979) in 1547.

[3] *LJ*, Introduction, pp. xx-xxi. Nosworthy supports his suggestion thus: "Albertus Magnus's *The Booke of Secretes,* licensed to King on 30 August 1560, that is a fortnight after the registration of *Lusty Juventus,* appeared under Copland's imprint, and this admits the possibility that both books were transferred simultaneously."

[4] *LJ*, Introduction, p. xxii.

[5] *LJ*, Introduction, p. xxii.

Dating in Relation to Theology: Henrician Theological Context

The significance of Wever's *Lusty Juventus* in the history of early Tudor drama is twofold: (1) it is a play of the religious transition between the old Catholic drama and the budding Reformation propaganda interludes, and (2) it is a play with considerable literary and dramatic artistry, which remained well known into the seventeenth century to such dramatists as Anthony Munday, Ben Jonson, Thomas Heywood, and probably Shakespeare. These two points will be examined at length in the pertinent sections of this Introduction, with greater emphasis being placed on the first since the examination of Wever's theological positions is necessary for an understanding of the play, while at the same time furnishing evidence for the dating of its composition to the reign of Henry VIII rather than to that of Edward VI as is traditional. Theologically it represents both a pulling back from the extreme reform advocated by Luther, Tyndale, Cromwell, Bale, and others (and temporarily countenanced by Henry VIII for political considerations), and an attempt to define the essential beliefs of the new English Church under its recently elevated royal head, now feeling the full responsibility of his new religious position.

An extensive comparison of the theology of the *King's Book* (1543), Henry VIII's statement of "Necessary Doctrine" for his subjects, and of Wever's *Lusty Juventus* will serve to place the interlude in the historical context of the theological eclecticism of Henry in the last years of his life, after the passage of the Act of Six Articles (1539) and the fall of Cromwell (1540).

In modern accounts of English Reformation drama, *Lusty Juventus* is invariably labeled an Edwardian morality play and usually dated around 1550, partly to correspond with the dates of the printer Abraham Vele's activities in London and partly to be consistent with the judgment of the eighteenth-century editor Thomas Hawkins that the play was written in the reign of Edward Sixth.[1] Hawkins' conjecture has been followed by subsequent editors and critics, including the editor of the 1971 Malone Society Reprint, J. M. Nosworthy, who cites Hawkins' evidence for the composition of the moral interlude: "a resemblance between the dialogue at lines 701-714 and a passage in the third of Latimer's seven Lenten sermons, preached before Edward VI in 1549(50) and published in that year."[2] Both Latimer and Wever present a young fellow saying that he may be drawn about the town with a pudding. The similarity of phrasing is used by Hawkins as evidence for concluding that Wever borrowed the phrase from Latimer and thus that the interlude must have been written after June of 1550, when the Lenten sermons were published. Nosworthy concedes that the story of the pudding may have been "in general currency" at the time, but nevertheless feels that the similarity of phrasing "offers powerful support to the supposition that *Lusty Juventus* was written sometime between the publication of Latimer's sermons, on or after 21 June 1550, and the death of the king on 6 July 1553" (p. xxii). He also thinks that it is clear "beyond reasonable doubt" that the play was written in the reign of Edward VI because he feels that the way in which the evangelical doctrine "is

DATING IN RELATION TO THEOLOGY   xv

combined with the theme of social redress reflects the outlook of Hugh Latimer, who may be assumed to have exerted a considerable influence on Wever" (p. xxi). But Latimer had preached evangelical sermons from the time of his conversion by Thomas Bilney in 1524 until his resignation of the Bishopric of Worcester in 1539 and could have exerted his influence on the author of *Lusty Juventus* long before the publication of his Edwardian sermons, and the "pudding" phrase could even have originated with Wever: Latimer was noted for his use of popular topical allusions.

David Bevington also accepts an Edwardian date for the interlude, drawing political inferences from the dating. Discussing the confusion arising from Henry VIII's period of "retrenchment" from religious reform in the years 1540-1547, Bevington judges Wever's play to be an Edwardian effort "to consolidate Protestant gains among the mass of perplexed Englishmen."[3] *Lusty Juventus,* he concludes, "ending with a direct appeal to Edward VI and the Protector, reflects both the zeal and the responsible caution of an erstwhile opposition now in power" (p. 107). But even with a consensus of critics, can the play really be dated with any certainty in the reign of Edward VI? The final prayer of what is judged to be the earliest extant printed text (the Vele edition) makes supplications to God to enable "our noble & vertuous king" to persevere in his "godly procedynges" which seek the glory of God above all things, and to "endue his hert, with true vnderstanding, / And geue him a prosperous life, long ouer vs to raigne" (ll. 1155-1159), but the name of the king is not given, nor is there a specific mention of the Protector. Actually the wording of the prayer would fit Henry VIII and his council as well as Edward VI and his, and, indeed, had to be altered only minimally for adaption to Queen Elizabeth and her council in the Copland and Awdely editions of the play, "king" being changed to "quene" and the pronouns, with one exception, adjusted to agree.

Nor can it be said that the supplication better suits Edward VI on the grounds that praying for Henry VIII to be granted a "prosperous life, long ouer vs to raigne" would be inappropriate for Henry in the last years of his reign. There are, indeed, just such supplications for this increasingly autocratic king in other records of the time.[4] Henry VIII was forty-six years old in August 1537 and only fifty-five when he died in January 1547. In the last ten years of his rule, it would certainly not have been out of order to pray for Henry to reign "long" over his subjects as the end of *Lusty Juventus* has it; in fact it might have been impolitic not to do so.

If it could be coincidence or the use of a commonplace that accounts for the similarity of the "pudding" phrasing in the interlude and in Latimer's sermon — or if, indeed, the borrowing could be from Wever to Latimer — and if the final supplication could have been originally intended for Henry VIII, there is no real evidence for dating the composition of the play to the reign of Edward. Even though Bevington concludes that Wever's interlude "typifies the Edwardian popular morality in its heavy emphasis on the political aspects of religious change" (p. 108), actually there is very little — nothing aside from the final prayer — that could be considered political in *Lusty Juventus*. More overtly political are John Bale's plays: *Three Laws*, for example, though published in the Edwardian period was "compiled" in the late 1530's and so is Henrician, as is *King John*, at least in its earliest version. Thus even if Wever's play were political, this fact would not necessarily place it in the reign of Edward VI. One moral interlude which can with certainty be dated as Edwardian, *John Bon and Mast Person* (to be discussed in some detail later), is not political at all.

A careful look at the internal evidence suggests that Wever's interlude is Henrician. The composition date is obviously after Henry VIII allowed the promulgation of the Bible in English (1537), since Good Councell refers to the joyful sight of Youth first embracing God's word as being in the past; just how many years after the momentous event is not certain, though it is long enough for the good counsellor to lament how little effect the availability of the scriptures has had on the moral and religious life of the people. Certainly, neither politically nor doctrinally is there anything in the play which would preclude its having been written in the last seven or eight years of the reign of Henry VIII — the period of so-called religious retrenchment under the prohibitions of the Act of Six Articles.

Wever's satire of "popish priests" — purveyors of ignorance, teachers of false doctrine, corrupters of God's word, and minions of the Deuyl's son Hypocrisie — might suggest an Edwardian date for the play; but throughout the later reign of Henry VIII, after the passage of the Act of Supremacy (1534), which declared the King supreme head of the Church of England, preachers, minstrels, and playwrights were permitted and even ordered and coerced to denounce the Pope and all popish idolatry.[5] The latter years of the reign saw charges brought against numerous clergymen for failing to preach against the usurped power of the Pope;[6] the Pope's name was systematically expunged from religious service books;[7] and abusive language about the Pope became common in letters to and from Henry VIII.[8]

Henry had spoken unrestrainedly in 1538 about the Pope's evils, his "subtleties," and the "sundry deceits, crafts, and subtleties of the Papists,"[9] and in 1543 his opinions had not changed as he was negotiating with his representative in Scotland for the extirpation of monks and friars, who spend "their time in all idleness and filthiness with such face of hypocrisy and superstition as is intolerable," and for the use of no books except scripture until such time as his own proper doctrine could be available to make both realms "in one understanding of God's word, 'whereby to eschew the fancies and dreams of the inferior people on the one side' and the corruption of hypocrisy and superstition maintained by the Bishop of Rome on the other."[10] Under the Pope's order of excommunication and fearing invasion from continental papal forces, Henry remained firm in his opposition to papal influence in England.[11]

A close analysis of the theology behind Wever's interlude indicates that the terms "Protestant" or "Lutheran" generally used for the play are imprecise and even misleading, as is the term "Edwardian." Theologically, *Lusty Juventus* actually fits best into the late Henrician-Protestant period.[12]

Although in recent years ecclesiastical historians have revealed how inaccurate the designation "religious retrenchment" is when applied to the last seven years of Henry's reign, literary historians have been slow to follow this revaluation. The Catholic historian Philip Hughes finds "little reality" in the "so-called 'Catholic' reaction supposed to have followed the disappearance from power of Cromwell [1540]. . . ."[13] A. F. Pollard had come to essentially the same conclusion early in this century: "the endeavour to stretch all his subjects on the Procrustean bed of Six Articles was one of Henry's least successful enterprises" and the idea of "a continuous and rigorous persecution" from 1539 to 1547 is a "legend derived from Foxe."[14] What the Whip of Six Strings did achieve, however, was the discouraging of overt attacks on the doctrinal matters covered in the Articles, especially against the mass as a sacrifice propitiatory and the doctrine of transubstantiation, attacks which did break out after the death of Henry VIII in great abundance. Wever's interlude, whether consciously or not, avoids all the doctrines covered in the Six Articles: transubstantiation and the real presence, communion in both kinds for the laity, marriage of priests, vows of chastity, private masses, and auricular confession. *Lusty Juventus* would not have offended Henry in any of these matters.

If Wever's text could not have been censored under this Act, was there any other official orthodoxy which would have made it dangerous to write *Lusty Juventus* in the last years of the reign of Henry VIII? Does Wever offend against the *Bishops' Book* of 1537 or its revision the *King's Book* of 1543, both of which present in great detail what to believe on the matter of Faith, the Creed, the Sacraments, the Pater Noster, Freewill, Justification, Good Works, and Prayers for departed souls?[15] There are differences in these two books of necessary doctrine, but Philip Hughes, writing as a Catholic historian, concludes that neither is really Lutheran and certainly neither is Catholic.[16] According to G. R. Elton, Henry VIII in his book "composed for himself an eclectic theology which varied his essential attachment to Catholic doctrine with some radical borrowings from the Protestants."[17] Wever's presentation of the key doctrines of faith, justification, good works, and penance agrees well enough with both the *Bishops' Book* and the *King's Book,* though he, too, is somewhat eclectic in the doctrine treated. His play may best be described as a late-Henrician Protestant work which avoided any major controversial elements in the "Royal Catholic" position of Henry VIII. That he omitted the doctrinal matters restricted in the Act of Six Articles is evident, but that his treatment of the central doctrines agrees with the letter and spirit of the official *King's Book* can be documented by a paralleling of the doctrinal elements in both works. From such documentation it will become evident that the interlude would not have disturbed the King's censors busy with strange heresies about the sacrament of the Altar, the real presence in the bread and wine, and the miracle of transubstantiation.[18]

Both Henry VIII and Wever recall the time when God's word in English was made available to the people — a reference either to the authorization of Matthew's Bible (1537) and the Royal Injunctions of 1538 which gave orders to place a copy "of the largest size" in every parish church, or possibly to the publication of the Great Bible in 1539. By 1543 Henry was disillusioned, perceiving that even "in the tyme of knowledge" the devil has attempted "to returne agayne . . . in to the hous purged & clensed, accompanied with seuen worse spirites," when, even with "hypocrisy and superstition" being excluded, some people still show "an inclination to sinister vnderstãdyng of scripture, presumption, arrogancy, carnal liberty, and contention . . ."; so he will set forth "suche a doctrine & declaration of the true knowledge of god and his word, with the principall articles of our religion, as wherby all mē may uniformely be ledde & taught the true vnderstandyng of that, whiche is necessary for euery christen man to know . . ." (sigs. A.ii-[A.ii^v]). Remembering what a "ioyful syght" it was "When Youth began Gods worde to embrace" (ll. 932-933), Wever dramatizes the falling away from virtue in the time of knowledge by the story of

Juventus, who is seduced by Hypocrisie, son of the Deuyl and personification of the continuing "hypocrisy and superstition" lamented by Henry VIII.

Wever's message and the King's are the same: know the true teachings of the word of God and live according to His precepts (Luke 11.28). Henry leaves the biblical passage in Latin but furnishes his own translation: "Blessed be they that here the true doctrine of god and keepe it . . ." (sig. [A.iii^v]), *verbum dei* being rendered "the true doctrine of god," which he says is the real meaning of the text. Wever's character Knowledge, actually labeled "The true Knowledge of Gods Veritie," following more closely the Latin text, utilizes the passage to instruct Juventus: "And Christ in the gospell sayth manyfestly, / Blessed is he which heareth the word of God & kepeth it" (ll. 201-202).

Both the King and dramatist complain about the moral conditions in England. In his Preface, Henry sorrowfully regrets the vices that remain in the hearts of his people. He was to be still crying out at the lack of charity and concord in his realm in his last speech before Parliament (1545), wherein he denounces the discord and dissension among the Lords Temporal and the Lords Spiritual and expresses his sorrow "to know and to hear how unreverently that most precious jewel, the Word of God, is disputed, rhymed, sung, and jangled in every Alehouse and Tavern" and to see how little virtuous living is in the land.[19]

Wever laments not only Youth's abandonment of God's word and testament, but also the general dissension and discord which infect every congregation (ll. 913-914). His character Good Councell, in an extended *ubi sunt* passage, asks where is now the godly "conuersation"; where are the "peace & mekenes, longe sufferinge & temperaunce / Which are the fruites of Gods holy spirit[?]" Who brings his flesh under obedience; who reads scripture with intent to follow it; who now is not given to covetousness and deceit; what parents set a good example for their children by "godly & vertuous liuing"; who thinks about the "dreadful rekenyng" that shall be required at judgment day (ll. 911-931).

Although Wever's short interlude could not hope to cover the full range of doctrine that Henry felt compelled to give his subjects in his "Necessary Doctrine for Any Christian Man," the play and the *King's Book* are in agreement on the doctrinal matters which Wever does manage to work into his brief account of the young man coming of age and facing the temptations of the World, the Flesh, and the Devil. On the important dogmas of faith, justification, and good works both authors are close theologically.

It is, in fact, remarkable how parallel are the King's and Wever's discussions of the nature of faith. For both, faith is a gift of God, something wrought by God in man's heart, or granted to him, but this beginning faith must "procede . . . to Hope and Charitie" to become a "lyuely faithe" which works to make man's will submissive to God's will: "And this is the effectual faythe, that worketh by charitie, which saint Paule vnto the Galathians affirmeth to be of value and strength in Christe Iesu" ("Gal. v." marginal gloss, *King's Book,* fol. [i^v]). Wever's character Good Councell urges Juventus to pray that God will "send" to him "his holy spirit and comforter" to lead him to "the knowledge of hys word and veritie" (ll. 152-154). The young man complies, asking God to "graunt" him the true knowledge of His law and will and to "illuminate" his heart with spirit continually so that he may perform good works and fulfill His precepts (ll. 156-159) to achieve a "perfite faith" (l. 214), which consists of the gift and the works which perfect it.

A corollary of their definition of the nature of faith is their agreement on the matter of justification: faith and works are necessary for man's justification. Both authors carefully avoid the Lutheran dogma of justification by faith alone, *fides sola:* Henry by insisting that beginning faith must proceed to works of charity to become a "lyuely" and "effectual faythe" (fol. [i^v]), and Wever by prefacing his statements that justification comes by faith in Christ's merits (ll. 220-221, 143-144) with admonitions about "Declaring the fayth by the fruites of the spirite" (ll. 201-204) and living according to God's commandments (ll. 119-122). On the other hand, both Henry and Wever deviate from the Catholic teaching on justification. Hughes sees Henry's use of the word "procede" as a wandering from the Catholic position: "A Catholic would say that hope and charity are, like faith, virtues infused into the soul when man is justified — and that it is normal, i.e., in the nature of supernatural life of man, that acts of faith believing God revealing, are concomitant with acts of hope trusting God our helper, and acts of charity loving God our friend" *(Reformation,* II, 53, n. 5). Writing for the laity, the King and the dramatist blur fine theological distinctions, separating faith and works but making both appear essential for justification.

Henry's theological ambivalence on the matter of justification may be illustrated by his contradictory statement that although good works — gifts of the holy ghost such as faith, repentance, hope, and charity — are necessary, "Yet it is to be vnderstande, that neuerthelesse we be iustified *Gratis*, that is to say frely, for as muche as all giftes or workes, wherby our iustification is wrought and accomplished, come of the free mercy and grace of god, and not of our deseruyng. . . . For we be not able of our selues, as of our selues, not as moche as to thinke any good thing" but our "ablenes" comes from God (fol. [lxxxix^v]). The ambiguity in this position on the necessity of good works is pinpointed by Hughes:

> The good acts [according to Henry] done in charity and in faith, of a man already reconciled to God, are in themselves "unperfect and insufficient"; but because these acts are "done in the faith of Christ," God "by the merits of [Christ's] passion," supplies "their unfulfilling of his law," and "they be . . . meritorious towards the attaining of everlasting life." Such works, it is said in a later passage, "are counted works of righteousness . . . by acceptation of God through Christ." This, again, although not the strict orthodoxy of Wittenberg, is yet far from the Catholic teaching about the real meritoriousness of such good acts.[20]

Cranmer, who had been Henry's adviser in the writing of his *Book*, admitted to Bishop Gardiner, after the King's death, that its language was ambiguous in statements about justification.[21]

Wever, too, shows vagueness on the matter of justification, fitting into neither the Lutheran nor the Catholic designation. Thus although his character Knowledge corrects Juventus' misconception about good works as means of justification (ll. 219-221), he also emphasizes that "where a perfite faith is, there is good workyng" (l. 214), adding that good works are required "As the necessary fruites of true repentaunce" (l. 225). Wever's perfect faith is a close cousin to Henry's lively faith which serves to make man submit to God's will and perform good works.

As to the nature of good works, both Henry and Wever define them as following God's commandments in a spirit of charity, and significantly both denounce the so-called good works of men's own invention. Henry insists:

> we meane not the supersticiouse workes of mennes own inuention, which be not commauded of god, nor approued by his worde, in which kind of workes many christen men and specially of them that were lately called religious (as monkes, friers, nunnes, and such other) haue in tymes past, put their great trust and confidence . . . but we speake of suche outwarde and inward workes, as god hath prepared for vs to walke in, and be done in the fayth of Christe, for loue & respecte of god, and can not be brought forth onely by mans

power, but must be preuented [preceded] and holpen therto by a special grace.

(King's Book, fol. [xc^v])

For Wever also, good works, proceeding from a perfect faith, are not the superstitious works which had blinded the parents of Juventus:

I know ryght well my elders and parentes,
Haue of a longe tyme deceyued be,
Wyth blynd hipocrisy and supersticyous ententes,
Trustyng in theyr owne workes which is nothyng but vanitie.

(ll. 256-259)

Closely related to their belief in the necessity of good works for justification is their rejection of the Lutheran dogma of double and immutable predestination — Henry explicitly, Wever implicitly. Henry specifically denounces the doctrine since he can find no scriptural references to it, concluding that though man is frail, he may achieve salvation by following the grace of god and perservering in godly living. Man ought not to trust to being predestined to salvation, but as scripture says, "we ought euermore to be in dread of our owne fraielty, and natural pronity to fall to synne, and not to assure our selfe, that we be elected any otherwise, than by feelyng of spiritual motions in our hart, and by tokens of good and vertuous liuyng, in following the grace of god, and perseueryng in the same to the ende . . ." (fol. lxxxix).[22] Wever implies his disagreement with the doctrine by indicating that man must live up to his part of the covenant in order to partake of the merciful promises of God to man, thus rejecting reprobation or election without regard to man's future merits. The subtitle of *Lusty Juventus* further implies a denial of immutable reprobation by describing "the frailtie of youth" as being "of nature, prone to vyce" but "by grace and good councell traynable to vertue." The parallel between Henry's phrase "natural pronity to fall to synne" and Wever's "of nature, prone to vyce," is striking, and neither author preaches the doctrine of predestination which Luther found comforting and Calvin, later, ineluctable.

On the all-important question of the way back after man has lapsed into sin, monarch and playwright are also in agreement. Both emphasize repentance which consists of an inward sorrow brought on by the preaching of the word of God — combining the threats for those who do not repent with the promises for those who do. Henry recommends that man prostrate himself before God to show his contrition, or penance, which must be understood as "an inwarde sorow and griefe of harte, for the synnes by vs done and commytted, and an hatred and detestation of the same, with an earnest desyre, to be purged from them, & to recouere agayne the grace and fauour of god, by suche meanes and remedies, as god hath appoynted for the obteyning therof, with a stedfast purpose & mynde neuer to offende agayne" and with a return to the battle against the temptations of the devil (fol. xxiii). Hughes sees Henry as managing "to combine a more or less traditional explanation of the sacrament of Penance, in the earlier part of his book, with an account of justification where only penance the virtue has a necessary role, and the sacrament of Penance is passed over entirely. . . ."[23] The process of returning to grace after sinning, says Hughes, "is the crucial matter where, for twenty-five years now, Luther has been so powerful and so revolutionary. . . . The King is surely here closer to Luther than to Fisher. Once again Henry, whatever he is, is not a Catholic."[24] Wever, if perhaps closer to Luther than Henry, is only a trifle so in omitting the sacramental path to repentance, along with the Catholic morality-play tradition of dramatizing the sacrament of Penance as the means whereby Humanum Genus or Everyman was turned away from sin and restored to grace.

The devil figures largely in Henry's *Book* as he does in Wever's interlude, where he is identified with the papists by his evident distress at finding his power abated since the young people refuse to live by "old traditions and made by man" (l. 343), choosing rather to follow the teachings of scripture. Henry is as much concerned with pointing out the wiles of man's crafty enemy as with spelling out necessary doctrine. The devil, he writes, is "the well and springe of iniquitie, and is not onely him selfe an homicide, a lyer, and an hater of the truthe from the begynning: but also is the very roote and occasion of al sinne, and the common prouoker and stirrer of man to the same, and the letter and hinderer of all vertue and goodnes, bycause this enemy neuer ceassith, but continually sercheth by all craftes & wiles to enduce vs to synne, and so to deuoure vs, and brynge vs therby to euerlastyng damnation" (fol. lxxxi). In Wever's play, this ancient enemy of man is on stage plotting to root out the word of God "clene from the heart of man" by turning the attention of youth to "carnall plesures" (ll. 333, 351). Doctrine is important, but it is more forceful if presented in a dramatic adversary situation with the devil on one side and God on the other as is done in both Henry's *Book* and Wever's drama.

As Wever's Deuyl is subtly identified with the papists, so is his son Hypocrisie, who has busied himself since the world began "To graffe [his father's] lawes in the heart of man," so mingling God's commandments with "vaine zeales, and blynd ententes, / That they be greatly abused" (ll. 397-401). Wever has Hypocrisie boastfully catalogue the "ydolatry," "filthy Sodometry," and "supersticion" which he has set up under the name of holiness and religion to deceive man (ll. 402, 403, 405). The boast, consisting of a listing of almost fifty "holy" items which associate this evil fellow with the papists or pope-Catholics (ll. 408-443), might seem at odds with the partial movement back towards conservatism in the last years of Henry's reign after the passage of the Act of Six Articles, but the holy things are said to be used for superstitious purposes — "Holy water, holy bread: / To driue away spirites," for example (ll. 430-431) — abuses which Henry had sought to eliminate even before his break with the Pope. In other cases the satire is directed against the Bishop of Rome and the regular clergy of the dissolved religious houses — permissible subjects of attack at all times after Henry became supreme head under God of the English Church.[25]

Henry's most often used epithets for the Pope are "hypocrisy" and "superstition," two words which occur frequently in *Lusty Juventus*. In fact, generally in Henrician literature after 1534 — in drama as well as the *King's Book* — these terms came to signify the Bishop of Rome, the papists, the monks, friars, and nuns of the former religious houses. John Bale, for instance, indicates that the character Hypocrisy in his play *Three Laws* is to be dressed like a grey friar, and the term "hypocrites" automatically means papists in his *The Chief Promises of God Unto Man* and *John the Baptist's Preaching in the Wilderness* ("compiled" 1538). When Henry is arguing against the authority of the Pope over the English Church, he charges that "by hypocrisy & usurpation" the Bishop of Rome has seized power and by means of superstitious abuses forced others to uphold and maintain that authority (fol. xvi).

These symbolic words are also to be seen in the art of the Henrician period: for example, in an illustrated edition of his *Book,* Henry's denunciation of the hypocrisy and superstition of the Bishop of Rome is accompanied by an almost full-page picture of a female figure wearing the triple crown of the Pope and riding on the Beast with Seven Heads, the Beast of the Apocalypse, while people, clergy, and kings kneel to her and look on.[26] Also, one of a series of anti-papal paintings recorded in Henry VIII's collection in 1542 depicts the Pope and his accomplices, Hypocrisy and Avarice, being vanquished by the Evangelists, while the true light of the gospel, symbolized by a lighted candle, triumphs. A cardinal's hat, indulgences, a holy water stoop, and a rosary can be seen beneath the Pope.[27]

For Wever, too, Hypocrisie is the instigator of papist superstitions and may even be seen as representing the Pope himself. When he hears his father the Deuyl calling him, he mistakes his voice for that of a hog vendor and offers to buy the sow since, as he says, he is a "bochare" [butcher] (l. 364) — a seemingly incongruous choice of occupation for this clever son of the Deuyl, which may, however, be illuminated by John Bale's designation of the Pope in *King Johan* as a "bloudy bocher" and "Beaste and slauterman of the deuyll," who has done much evil against Christian princes.[28]

There is some indication in Wever's interlude that Juventus might be in danger from his vigorous professing of God's word, speaking out for it in public places (ll. 623-630). Such a hint may refer to the attempt made by Henry in 1543 to limit the reading of the English Bible to the upper classes and to his openly regretting, as later in his 1545 parliament speech, the familiar way in which the common people discussed, rhymed, and sang the scriptures in ale houses and taverns. As we have seen, the King issued his *Book* because he had found in some of his people "an inclination to sinister vnderstādyng of scripture" (Preface). The common people were enjoined to read and print the official "Necessary Doctrine" in their hearts, but as for reading the Bible, the King says, since God has ordered some men to teach and some to be taught, those who are ordered to teach should and must read the Old and New Testaments, whereas for those who are designated to be taught, reading the scriptures is not necessary, except as the prince allows it (Preface, sig. [A.iii^v]). Although Juventus' owning a New Testament, even if not specifically Tyndale's (prohibited in statutes and proclamations of 1543 and 1546),[29] might seem dangerous in the light of the restriction of 1543 on the reading of the scriptures by the common people,[30] a close examination of Wever's play reveals that for the most part the young protagonist *hears* the true doctrine and the scriptural passages from the mouth of the good counsellors, who quote or paraphrase for him. Thus there is little reason to think that the drama would offend on this score. What Henry had hoped to avoid by limiting scripture reading can be illustrated by the recantation of one Robert Warde, who expressed his penitence "that he, being a man of small experience and no learning, has taken upon himself in ale houses and other places (chiefly when overcome with ale) to expound the Scripture. . . ."[31] Juventus is never guilty of such indiscretion.

A comparison of the *King's Book* and Wever's play places *Lusty Juventus* firmly in the theological context of the pre-Edwardian Reformation. The work, moreover, contains nothing in the way of doctrinal matters which would result in serious charges of heresy during the late Henrician years on the nature of faith, justification, good works, or penance. Records of examinations of people called before the authorities for heresy indicate no concern for these matters. Predominantly, the charges in 1540, 1543, and 1546 were for denying the real presence of the body and blood of Christ in the sacrament of the Altar. There were other accusations in the years 1540-1547 — speaking out against auricular confession and ordination as a sacrament, for example — but the denial of the real presence in the eucharist was the most common.[32] Wever does not speak to this issue.

After the death of Cromwell in 1540, Archbishop Cranmer continued to hold the line and to protect the preachers of the "new learning" in his diocese. Opposition to his policies, however, gained strength and came to a head with the burning of three men from Windsor accused of proscribed teachings on the sacrament of the Altar (July 1543) and with the preparation of articles of accusation against the Archbishop.[33] But the winds changed again when on July 12, 1543, Henry married Catherine Parr, and charges of Protestant heresy made against personages of the court and royal household were intercepted and privately investigated, the accused being pardoned without mention of abjuration. Cranmer was allowed to investigate the charges against himself, received apologies from his accusers, and was given no punishment.[34] The publication of the *King's Book* in 1543 might seem to be a repudiation of all that Cranmer had worked for, writes Hughes, but actually it was not, since the doctrine of Henry's *Book* represented a move toward Lutheranism and away from pure Catholicism.[35] The reform elements in Henry's "Royal Catholicism" of 1543 make it probable that *Lusty Juventus* was a product of the waning years of his long reign.

Wever's play might well be related to the 1542 Injunctions of Bishop Bonner ordering alehouse keepers not to suffer ungodly gatherings (such as that of Hypocrisie, Juventus, and the girl Abhominable Liuing): "By a detestable custom universally reigning, young people and other ill-disposed persons, on Sundays and Holy days, in time of divine service and preaching, resort to ale houses and there exercise unlawful games 'with great swearing, blasphemy, drunkenness, and other enormities.'"[36]

The interlude would have been especially topical in the year 1544 which saw the publication of *A Supplicacion to our moste Soueraigne Lorde Kynge Henry Eyght*.[37] As does Wever, the anonymous author of the *Supplicacion* laments the ignorance and blindness of the realm, attributing the decay to the "lacke of knowledge in Gods Worde" among the people, caused by the clergy, who had spent their time in subtle disputes instead of preaching the truth of the word of God to the people (p. 22). Both authors go to Isaiah 5 to find the cause of evil in the land; both emphasize popish blindness.[38] In a style reminiscent of Wever's, the *Supplicacion* condemns the clergy for teaching that holiness stands "in their holy oyle / , holy creame / , holy water / , holy asshes / , hallowed bedes / . . . ."[39] It also complains, as does *Lusty Juventus* (ll. 999-1001), about the emphasis on fashionable dress and about the vices of the people: "manyfolde and dyuerse chaunges of fasshyons," along with "detestable swearinge," pride, covetousness, and all other "detestable vyce," that plague the land (pp. 52-53). The *Supplicacion* closes with a petition to the Lord for Henry VIII, asking that the King be made to know and to redress the abuses exposed in the tract, thus illustrating specifically the nature of the complaints for which redress is sought in Wever's final supplication (ll. 1154-1167).

If, as seems likely, Wever's interlude was written at about the same time as the *Supplicacion,* published in 1544 in Antwerp, why was it not printed until several years later? The delay may have had something to do with the state of printing in the final years of Henry's reign, which, as Edward Gordon Duff points out, "were an unsettled period for printers," who "themselves seemed hardly to know what might or might not be printed and even the most important were continually in trouble."[40] Concerning the unspecified and uncertain date of printing of *Lusty Juventus,* however, all that can be said is that the datable activities of the first printer, Abraham Vele, began in 1547 and were thus post-Henrician. We do not know how the play came into the hands of the printer, and the question of when the play was first published may not be a significant one. Delay in the printing of plays (or, for that matter, lack of a printed text altogether) is, of course, a common and unremarkable phenomenon.

There were, to be sure, attempts to regulate the performance of certain plays in addition to the publishing of books. It is known that the papists as well as the reformers used the stage for religious propaganda, as is indicated by a letter of Henry VIII to a justice of the peace in the north of England complaining about the seditious interludes performed by papists, which resulted in "the late and seditious rising in our ancient city of York," and ordering the "apprehending and putting in prison [of] any papists who shall, in performing interludes which are founded on any portions of the Old or New Testament, say or make use of any language which may tend to excite those who are beholding the same to any breach of the peace."[41] And in 1542, the bishops in Convocation at Canterbury requested the King to "correct the public plays and comedies which are acted in London, to the contempt of God's Word. . . ."[42] What these plays were is not recorded, but such a request could in no way apply to Wever's interlude, which extols the significant role of the word of God.

Dating in Relation to Theology: Edwardian Theological Context

In the attempt to determine whether *Lusty Juventus* suits better the Henrician than the Edwardian period, references to Cranmer's *Book of Homilies,* July 1547 (six months after the death of Henry), may be helpful. Even though the *King's Book* was not officially discarded as a guide to orthodoxy until 1548, it was essentially superseded by Cranmer's sermons, ordered to be read Sunday after Sunday to all congregations.[43] In the homilies on faith, justification, and good works, Cranmer's *Book,* differing in tone from the *King's Book* and from Wever's presentation, represents a significant further movement towards Lutheran dogma. Frequent repetition of such phrases as justification by "faith onely" and "Christ onely" leaves no doubt about the radical bent of the sermons on salvation and good works.[44] That the *Homilies* were Lutheran in emphasis is attested to by the expressed opposition to them by Bishop Gardiner in letters to Cranmer in 1548, his first reason of protest being that these homilies teach a doctrine that is in plain contradiction to that of the *King's Book* — that "only faith justifieth."[45] He maintained that Cranmer's sermon on justification says that whoever denies this doctrine "is not to be reputed a true Christian man," a "terrible slander" on King Henry, who according to Gardiner certainly denied the doctrine and ordered that the denial be taught as part of the necessary doctrine.[46] Wever's stance on this doctrine, closer to that of Henry VIII than to Cranmer's in the Edwardian period, suggests a Henrician ambience for the play.[47]

Other evidence for considering *Lusty Juventus* pre-Edwardian may be found in the outburst of writings and publications attacking the Catholic Mass in the years 1547-1550 — dialogues and treatises which were not tolerated in the reign of Henry VIII. Since Wever takes no notice of this violent explosion of public religious controversy over the issues of Communion in both kinds for the laity, the mass as a sacrifice, the real presence in the elements of the eucharist, and the doctrine of transubstantiation, his play seems better suited to the last years of Henry's reign.

Henry's death made possible the reappraisal of the Act of Six Articles. The Parliament of November 1547 sanctioned Communion in both kinds for the people and in doing so adopted a practice which was considered heretical by implication even though there was no actual denial of the real presence.[48] The attacks on the mass as a sacrifice multiplied; the extent of the controversy is attested to by the Royal Proclamation, issued December 27, 1547, which sought with little success to prohibit all discussion of the real presence of Christ's body and blood in the sacrament except by learned men.[49] But by August of 1548, indeed, the official political opinion was changing to fit the times, and Cranmer himself made a public declaration against the real presence in a disputation before the House of Lords, and nobles of the Council were in agreement with his position.[50] This official stand had already essentially been affirmed in the *Order of Communion,* March 8, 1548, where English was to be used for the first time for administration of the sacrament; and the *Order,* by its wording, gave leave for the people to deny the real presence.[51] This position was reaffirmed by the first *Book of Common Prayer,* January 21, 1549.[52] Wever's apparent lack of awareness of these momentous events — the *Order,* the *Book of Common Prayer,* the violent western revolts which followed the attempt to force the people to abandon their mass in Latin, and the raging battle over the mass itself[53] — suggests an earlier religious context for *Lusty Juventus.*

Especially significant for a study of *Lusty Juventus* is the Edwardian play entitled *The Enterlude of John Bon & Mast Person; A Dialogue on the Festival of Corpus Christi, and on Transubstantiation,*[54] whose subject is what would be expected in this open season on the doctrine of transubstantiation, the corporeal presence of Christ's body and blood in the elements of the eucharist, and the mass as a sacrifice propitiatory. It is a debate between Master Person and the crafty John Bon, ploughman, on the real presence and the doctrine of the substantial change in the elements of the sacrament, set against the Corpus Christi Procession. About the parson's claim that the priest turns the bread and wine into flesh and blood with five words, John is skeptical: "The deuell ye do! I trowe. Ther is pestilence busines!" (p. 20). He remains unconvinced, maintaining that though he has "no learning" he knows "chese from chalke" (p. 22). The interlude is topical for this period of propaganda against the Catholic doctrine underlying the mass, as *Lusty Juventus* is not. There is even a critical mention of Cranmer's *Catechism,* published in June 1548, as currently giving comfort to the Catholic position, ironic in light of Cranmer's speech to the contrary in August of that year.

The accusations in the fusillade of popular attacks on the Catholic Mass, the doctrine of transubstantiation, and the corporeal presence in the elements of the eucharist were repeated and substantiated with great scholarship by Cranmer in *A Defence of the True and Catholic Doctrine of the Sacrament of the Body and Blood of Our Saviour Christ,*[55] published in 1550. His attack on the papists' Mass and the doctrine of transubstantiation is as acrid as any of the prior ones, Book IV of the *Defence* stressing the physical horror and repugnance of anthropophagy, which he sees following from the belief in the presence of the "very natural body of Christ" in the sacrament where it is "broken and torn in pieces with our teeth" (pp. 77-78). Cranmer's position on the "True" doctrine of the sacrament avoided Luther's insistence on the corporeal presence, as well as Zwingli's contention that the sacrament is only commemorative and symbolic, and was essentially that being promulgated by Calvin — that there is a spiritual presence in the administration of the sacrament and that the elements are not mere signs or tokens. As a result of this theological affirmation, the year 1551 saw the issuance of an order to replace all altars with tables since the form of a table would "move the simple [people] from the superstitious opinions of the Popish Mass unto the right use of the Lord's Supper."[56]

The second *Book of Common Prayer,* 1552, also broadly Calvinistic, was a really revolutionary departure from the first, marking "the full arrival of the Protestant Reformation" and setting "the crown on Cranmer's work."[57] With the death of Edward VI in July of 1553, however, the period of rapid progression of religious reform came to an abrupt end in the reinstatement of the Catholic Mass and service books under Queen Mary.

Those truly drastic changes in the religious scene characterize the milieu in England from the death of Henry VIII in January 1547 to the accession of his Catholic daughter, a context not at all mirrored in Wever's *Lusty Juventus.*[58] The play does reflect the climate of the last years of Henry's reign, years of moderate reform in areas not covered by the Act of Six Articles.

Notes

[1]*The Origin of the English Drama, Illustrated in its various species, viz. Mystery, Morality, Tragedy, and Comedy, by specimens from our earliest writers* (Oxford: Clarendon, 1773), I, [115].

[2]*Lusty Juventus* (Oxford: Univ. Press for the Malone Society, 1971), p. xxi.

³*Tudor Drama and Politics, A Critical Approach to Topical Meaning* (Cambridge, Mass.: Harvard Univ. Press, 1968), pp. 106-107. Others dating the play in the reign of Edward VI include Peter J. Houle, *The English Morality and Related Drama, A Bibliographical Survey* (Hamden, Conn.: Shoe String Press, 1972), p. xxx; F. P. Wilson, *The English Drama, 1485-1585* (New York and Oxford: Univ. Press, 1969), p. 39; A. P. Rossiter, *English Drama from Early Times to the Elizabethans: Its Background, Origins, and Development* (1950; rpt. New York: Barnes & Noble, 1967), p. 133; W. Roy Mackenzie, *The English Moralities from the Point of View of Allegory* (Boston and London: Ginn, 1914), p. 95; and Charles Mills Gayley, *Representative English Comedies* (New York: Macmillan, 1912), I, lxxiii. The one exception to dating *Lusty Juventus* as Edwardian is Richard Southern's. He somewhat hesitatingly concludes that perhaps it is from an earlier period, writing thus about the line in which Good Councell accuses Juventus of cutting and jagging his clothes: "The interest lies in the fact that jagging was not used as a form of decoration after about 1475: it would thus seem to have been a curious accusation to make in the mid-sixteenth century, and it suggests that the play is at least an adaptation of an older one, if it is not in fact itself ascribable to an earlier date than 1550." *(The Staging of Plays Before Shakespeare* [London: Faber and Faber, 1973], p. 360.)

⁴A specific example occurs in the anonymous play *Thersites*, which ends with Miles, a knight, calling on the audience to obey God and their king and to pray for the king "That long he may rule us without grief or pain." Although Henry VIII is not named, specific mention is made of his queen, "Lovely Lady Jane," and the prince that God has sent them, allowing for the precise dating of this play since Prince Edward was born 12 August 1537 and Queen Jane Seymour died soon thereafter. *(A Select Collection of Old English Plays,* ed. W. Carew Hazlitt [1874-76; rpt. New York: Benjamin Blom, 1964], p. 431.) Cf. the similar supplication for Henry VIII, 1543, in the Record Office of the House of Lords in a provision added at the end of the Statute of Proclamations: "This act to endure during the King's majesty's life which our Lord long preserve," quoted by R. W. Heinze, *The Proclamations of the Tudor Kings* (Cambridge and London: Cambridge Univ. Press, 1976), p. 176. In 1544, John Heywood, in his recantation, prays for "the long and most prosperous estate of our Soueraign Lord and Kings Majesty in all his affairs and proceedings," quoted by Robert W. Bolwell, *The Life and Works of John Heywood* (New York: Columbia Univ. Press, 1921), p. 162. Even in 1546 there is a sup-

plication to the Lord that he bring Henry's enemies to confusion, "geuyng your Highnes long lyfe, with assistence of hys grace, to performe that whyche you haue begonne. . . ." *(A Supplication of the Poore Commons,* 1546, reprinted in *Four Supplications, 1529-1553 A.D.,* ed. J. M. Cowper, EETS, ES, No. 13 [London: for the Early English Text Society, 1871], p. 92.)

[5]From 1535-1540, Cromwell took charge of the offensive against the Bishop of Rome, making sure that the right things were said from the pulpits and creating "an interlocking structure of supervision and control." The Pope's name was to be erased out of all service books; some clergy sought to evade the order "by pasting pieces of paper over the title" and were severely punished for the attempted evasion (G. R. Elton, *Reform and Reformation, England, 1509-1558* [Cambridge, Mass.: Harvard Univ. Press, 1977], p. 196). See also *Letters of the Kings of England,* ed. James Orchard Halliwell (London: Henry Colburn, Publisher, 1848), I, 343, for letter to judges to cause all manner of prayers, rubrics, and canons in service books "wherin the said bishop [of Rome] is named, to be utterly abolished, eradicate, and razed out in such wise as the said bishop of Rome, his name, and memory, for evermore (except unto his contumely and reproach) may be extinct, suppressed, and obscured. . . ."

[6]For examples see *Letters and Papers, Foreign and Domestic, of the Reign of Henry VIII,* Vol. XVIII, Pt. 2, 1543, No. 546, "Cranmer and the Heretics of Kent." Further references to this series will be indicated by *LP.*

[7]For examples see *LP,* Vol. XVII, 1542, No. 176, which reports on the move in Convocation by the Archbishop of Canterbury for the abolishing of candles before images and more diligent erasing of the names of the bishops of Rome and Thomas Becket from service books; also see Vol. XVIII, Pt. 2, 1543, Nos. 546 and 479.

[8]Paget to Henry VIII reports (February 1542) on a visit to the Queen of Navarre, who says that "the Emperor is hypocrisy and the Pope the Devil" and that she and Henry agree on matters of religion; Morryson to Henry VIII proposes "a yearly memorial of the destruction of the bp of Rome out of the realm, as the victory of Agincourt is annually celebrated at Calais. . . . It would be better that the plays of Robin Hood and maid Marian should be forbidden, and others devised to set forth and declare lively before the people's eyes the abomination and wickedness of the bishop of Rome, monks, friars, nuns, and such like, and to declare the obedience due to the King." *(LP,* Vol. XVII, 1542, No. 128 and Appendix, No. 2.)

Henry's letters to Lord Mordaunt call the Bishop of Rome "the pestilent idol, enemy of all truth, and usurpator of princes" who seeks to rob and spoil England and "invert the good religion," urging Lord Mordaunt to arrest any who seduce the people into false belief in the authority of the Bishop of Rome in order to bring the people to quietness and "to a perfection and knowledge of the mere verity and truth, and no longer to be seduced nor blinded with such superstitions and false doctrine of an earthly usurper of God's law." *(Letters of the Kings of England,* ed. James Orchard Halliwell [London: Henry Colburn, 1848], I, 359-360, 362; hereafter cited Halliwell, *Letters.)*

[9]Halliwell, *Letters,* I, 373.

[10]Quoted in *LP,* Vol. XVIII, Pt. 1, 1543, No. 364.

[11]The year 1544 saw Henry, at war with France and fearing the alliance between France and Scotland, still firm against the Pope's authority. See *LP,* Vol. XIX, Pt. 1, 1544, No. 853, for account of the recantation of John Heywood, Wever's fellow dramatist, for his blindness in accepting the usurped power of the Bishop of Rome. See also *LP,* Vol. XIX, Pt. 2, 1544, Nos. 134 and 135 for Henry as schismatic king and enemy of the Church; and *LP,* Vol. XX, Pt. 1, 1545, Nos. 28, 91, 667, 669; Pt. 2, 1545, No. 914.

[12]But one must also distinguish between "Henrician-Catholic" and "Henrician-Protestant," and further between early and late "Henrician-Catholic" as well as early and late "Henrician-Protestant." Henry's own theology in the early years of his reign was orthodox Roman Catholicism, but during the years after 1533 could be termed "Royal Catholicism," A. F. Pollard's term for Henry's religion after the break with Rome *(Thomas Cranmer and the English Reformation 1489-1556* [1902; rpt. New York: G. P. Putnam's Sons, 1906], p. 125). Also the Protestant Reformation movement of the Henrician era must be divided into the free and open reform allowed between 1533-1539 and the somewhat restricted reform carried on by Cranmer after the enactment of the Act of Six Articles in 1539.

[13]Philip Hughes, *The Reformation in England* (London: Hollis & Carter, 1953), II, 13.

[14]A. F. Pollard, *Henry VIII* (1902; rpt. London and Harlow: Longmans, Green, 1968), p. 321. There were, Pollard writes, "outbursts of rigour in 1540, 1543, and 1546, but except for these the Six Articles remained almost a dead letter" (p. 321, n. 1).

[15]The *King's Book* was titled *A Necessary Doctrine and Ervdition for Any Christen man, sette furthe by the kynges maiestie of Englande . . .* Imprinted

at London in Fletestrete by Thomas Barthelet printer to the kynges hyghnes, the .xxix. day of May, the yere of our Lorde .M.D.XLIII. *Cvm priuilegio ad imprimendum solum* (Colophon). It was Henry's revision (with Cranmer's aid) of *The institvtion of a Christen man, conteynynge the Exposytion or Interpretation of the commune Crede, of the seuen Sacramentes, of the .x. commandementes, and of the Paternoster, and the Aue Maria, Iustyfication & Purgatory.* Londini, in aedibvs Thomae Bertheleti, 1537 *(STC* 5163), known as the *Bishops' Book.* All further references to the *King's Book* are to *STC* 5168 (unless otherwise indicated), which has only signature numbers in the Preface but which is foliated in the text proper.

[16] *Reformation,* II, 55-56.

[17] *Reform,* p. 301. Elton cites J. J. Scarisbrick, *Henry VIII* (Berkeley and Los Angeles: Univ. of California Press, 1968), Ch. 12.

[18] The records show them concerned with Anabaptists and Sacramentaries, with those who were "of the Sadducee opinion, denying the resurrection of Christ in his manhood, saying, that He rose only in Spirit," or with others who maintained that "Christ was nourished with celestial milk and not material," or that "God did ingrave the whole power and wisdom of the Trinity in Lucifer," or that "the Bible was made by the devil," and so on, with an incredible proliferation of heresies to be combated. See *LP,* Vol. XVIII, Pt. 2, 1543, No. 546, pp. 318, 317, 293, and 296.

[19] Quoted by Pollard, *Henry VIII,* p. 337.

[20] *Reformation,* II, 57.

[21] Hughes, *Reformation,* II, 89, gives a detailed account of Gardiner's letters. The interchange took place in 1547 after the publication of Cranmer's *Book of Homilies,* which Gardiner objected to as teaching against the *King's Book* that "only faith justifieth."

[22] Hughes concludes, "if it [this statement] avoids the fundamental Luther and will satisfy those who detest the heresiarch, [it] gives yet a strong hope to the new believers in inner light and private inspiration." *(Reformation,* II, 56.)

[23] *Reformation,* II, 56.

[24] *Reformation,* II, 55-56.

[25] In 1543 there were numerous official charges against clergymen in Kent for the same matters which Wever includes in his satire of papists, especially against clerics for not declaring to the people the true (Anglican) meaning of the ceremonies and the correct use of holy water and holy bread, of hallowed candles, ashes, palms, and creeping to the cross *(LP,*

Vol. XVIII, Pt. 2, 1543, No. 546, "Cranmer and the Heretics," *passim*).

[26]*A Necessary Doctrine and erudition for any christen man, sette forthe by the kynges maieste of England,* 1543. Imprynted at Londō in Botulphe lane at the sygne of the whyte Beare by Iohn Mayler. *Ad imprimendum solum.* (Colophon, n. d.) *STC* 5175. Sigs. [D. vii-D. vii^v]. The illustration is accompanied by the warning: "This vsurpacion before rehearsed wel considered, it may appere, that the Bysshop of Rome, dothe contrarye to Goddis lawe, in chalengynge superioritie and preeminence, by a cloke of goddis lawe ouer all: And yet to make an apparaunce, that it shuld be soo he hath and doth wreste scriptures for that purpose, contrary both to the true meanyng of the same, and the interpretation of ancient doctours of the churche, so that by that chalenge he wolde not do wronge onelye to thys Churche of Englande, but also to al other churches, in clayminge, this superiorytye, wythoute anye aucthorite by god, so to him gyuen. . . ."

[27]Reproduced by Roy Strong, *Painting in England, 1540-1620: The Elizabethan Image.* An exhibition organized by the Tate Gallery, 28 Nov. 1969 - 8 Feb. 1970 (New York: Arno, 1969), p. 8. It is titled "The Four Evangelists stoning the Pope," and is based according to Strong, on a woodcut in the 1536 Bible depicting the stoning of the blasphemous man, by Girolamo da Treviso, one of a number of Italian artists in the service of Henry VIII. Other paintings "showed Truth unveiling the iniquities of the Pope and Henry VIII wielding the sword, inscribed *Verbum Dei,* trampling on the Pope as the beast of the Apocalypse" (p. 13).

[28]Ed. Barry B. Adams (San Marino, Cal.: The Huntington Library, 1969), ll. 2407, 2417. Later in the century, 1581, Nathaniel Woodes, in *The Conflict of Conscience,* picked up this early tradition and showed Sathan appointing Hypocrisie to be his agent to check the enemies of the Pope, Sathan's "darlyng deare . . . and his eldest boy," in whom he takes great delight.

[29]*LP,* Vol. XVII, 1542, No. 177. The draft of the proclamation being undated, the editors have placed it in this volume. For a correct dating of the proclamation and its relation to the Parliamentary Act regulating Printing, see Heinze, *Proclamations,* pp. 188-199 and also *LP,* Vol. XXI, Pt. 1, 1546, No. 1233; also *LP,* Vol. XVIII, Pt. 1, 1543, No. 66(6), and for examples of enforcement of the restrictions, see Nos. 384, 431, and 454.

[30]*LP,* Vol. XVIII, Pt. 1, 1543, Nos. 66(6) and 846 for restrictions on Bible reading. The confusion about Bible reading can be illustrated by conflicting charges against clergy in Kent in 1543. Against one "popish" priest was made the charge that he discouraged men from reading the

Bible, saying, "You fellows of the new trickery that go up and down with your Testaments in your hands, I pray you what profit take you by them?" There was a deposition against one clergyman that he commanded "that no man should read or hear the Bible read on pain of imprisonment," and that he "cast two in prison, the one for speaking against him" in this matter and "the other for showing him the King's injunctions concerning" Bible reading. On the other hand, there were accusations against a layman for reading the Bible in English aloud in church to his wife and others. *(LP,* Vol. XVIII, Pt. 2, 1543, No. 546, "Cranmer and the Heretics.")

[31]*LP,* Vol. XIX, Pt. 2, 1544, No. 805.
[32]*LP,* Addenda, Vol. I, Pt. II (sic), 1538-1547, No. 1463.
[33]Hughes, *Reformation,* II, 17-18. See also Pollard, *Henry VIII,* pp. 320-325.
[34]Hughes, *Reformation,* II, 19-20.
[35]Hughes, *Reformation,* II, 55-57.
[36]*LP,* Vol. XVII, 1542, No. 282.
[37]Reprinted in *Four Supplications, 1529-1553 A.D.* All further references to this work appear in the text.
[38]"For through the want of preachyng Godes Worde synce[re]lly, haue entered in all popyshe blyndnes / , vayne & dead ceremonyes / ; mennes tradycyons be crept into the conscyences of the symple innocentes, in the steade of the lawe of God. Yea, ydolatrye, and all hypocryse, with detestable superstycyon, for lacke of the lyght of Godes Worde / , is become Gods [sic] seruyce." *(Supplicacion,* p. 26.) Cf. *Lusty Juventus,* ll. 604-606, 256-259, and 247-248, for Wever's similar analysis.
[39]P. 41. This cataloguing technique reminds us of Wever's in his listing of holy items in Hypocrisie's long boast; it is used again when the king's realm is said to be overburdened with "the greate multytude of chauntery prestes / , soule prestes / , chanons / , resydensaryes in chatedrall churches / , prebendaryes / , muncke pencyons / , morowe mas prestes / , vnlerned curates / , prestes of gyldes and of fraternytees, or brotherhedes / , rydinge chaplaynes / and suche other ydle parsons . . ." *(Supplicacion,* p. 42).
[40]*A Century of the English Book Trade* (London: for the Bibliographical Society, 1905), p. xxiv.
[41]Halliwell, *Letters,* I, 354.
[42]*LP,* Vol. XVII, 1542, No. 176. And in April of 1543, "three joiners named Hawtrell, Lucke, and Lucas who were, for an unlawful disguising, committed to the tower, were released. . . ." *(LP,* Vol. XVIII, Pt. 1, 1543,

Nos. 392 and 463, "Business of the Privy Council.")

[43]Pollard terms this Cranmer's *Book of Homilies,* but it is not certain how many of them he actually authored. According to Pollard, Cranmer had begun work on these sermons as early as 1539 *(Cranmer,* p. 166; see also *LP,* Vol. XIV, Pt. 1, 1539, No. 466), but it was not until 1543 that the homilies were submitted to, but not approved by, Convocation *(LP,* Vol. XVIII, Pt. 1, 1543, No. 167).

[44]*Certaine Sermons or Homilies Appointed to be Read in Churches in the Time of Queen Elizabeth* (1547-1571). A facsimile reproduction of the edition of 1623 with an introduction by Mary Ellen Rickey and Thomas B. Stroup (Gainsville, Fla.: Scholars Facsimilies & Reprints, 1968), pp. 15-18. For example, the short second part of the sermon on salvation repeats such "onely" phrases sixteen times in addition to frequent repetition of the variation "iustified freely." The significant reiteration gives a strong feeling of *fides sola.*

[45]Hughes, *Reformation,* II, 92.

[46]Hughes, *Reformation,* II, 92-93.

[47]Another important event, coinciding with the appearance of the *Homilies* in 1547, was the publication of an official translation of Erasmus' *Paraphrases* of the Gospel, coupled with an order to the clergy to study and to provide a copy of them to be placed in the church for use of the parishioners (Hughes, *Reformation,* II, 92). Although Erasmus remained an avowed Catholic to his death, his works were looked upon with disfavor by the Church and later placed on the Index by the Council of Trent. The Protestant reformers, on the other hand, espoused them. Wever shows no awareness of this significant movement to the left.

[48]Jasper Ridley, *Thomas Cranmer* (Oxford: Clarendon, 1962), p. 272. Ridley makes this judgment about the resolution passed by Convocation which preceded the Parliamentary Act and resulted in the offering of Communion in both kinds to the people.

[49]Ridley, *Cranmer,* p. 275.

[50]Ridley, *Cranmer,* p. 284.

[51]In Hughes' words, "in the manner of speech [in the *Order*] about the presence of our Lord in the sacrament there are ambiguities designed to make the rite one which could be conscientiously used by those who did not believe that He was there present except to the communicant in the moment of receiving Holy Communion, and who believed that the presence, even at that moment, was not in what was received but only 'in the heart' of the receiver." *(Reformation,* II, 102.)

[52] Ridley, *Cranmer*, p. 287.

[53] See Ridley, *Cranmer*, Ch. XIX, for an account of these revolts. A sampling of the onslaught of vituperative attacks on the Catholic Mass in the first half of the Edwardian period will suffice to indicate the nature and extent of this outbreak of pent-up emotion which swept the country after Henry's death. Some were dignified and reasoned in approach: see, for example, the anonymous *Dyalogue of Disputaciō bytwene a Gentylman and a Prest Concernyng the Supper of y̆ Lorde (STC* 6800 [Hans Hilprick? 1547?]). Others were violently antagonist and even scurrilous in tone: see for examples, William Turner's *A newe dialogue wherin is conteyned the examinatiō of the messe (STC* 24362-24364 [1548? 1550?]), which sets out to demonstrate in a court trial that Mastres Missa is "of Anti-Christ" and "but a fained thing, to win money w̆ to [sic] the idle priests that can not preach" (sigs. [A.viii-A.viii^v]); the anonymous poem *The vpcheringe of the messe (STC* 17630 [1547?]); and William Punt's *A New Dialoge called the endightment agaynste mother Messe (STC* 20499 1548) in which "Mother Messe" is accused of being worse than Judas, and all Christian men are warned to beware of "thys wycked sprite for she is the rosse coloread whore that sainct John spake of In hys reuylaciōs . . ." (sigs. [B.iii^v] and [C.iiii^v]).

[54] Ed. from the black letter edition by William Henry Black (London: for the Percy Society, 1852). This *Enterlude* was originally printed "at London, by John Daye, and Willyam Seres, dwellinge in Sepulchres Parishe, at the Signe of the Resurrection, a littel above Holbourne Conduite. *Cum gratia et privilegio ad imprimendum solum.*" No date is given for its publication but since it mentions Cranmer's *Catechism*, published June 1548, it must postdate this work. All further references to this interlude are in the text.

[55] Reprinted in *The Work of Thomas Cranmer*, introd. J. I. Packer and ed. G. E. Duffield (Philadelphia: Fortress, 1965), pp. 45-231. All further references to the *Defence* are in the text, hereafter cited Duffield, *Cranmer*.

[56] Duffield, *Cranmer*, p. 235.

[57] Elton, *Reform*, pp. 365-366.

[58] Virginia Stuart Kelly (*"Lusty Juventus*, A Study in Lutheran Drama," M. A. Thesis Fordham University 1944) quotes Good Councell's reprimand of Juventus for his sinful life (ll. 947-949), and maintains that the term "fleshly Capernite . . . definitely connects Wever's play with the Transubstantiation controversy" (p. 57), since the word "Capernite . . .

was a well-known expression of contempt for a believer in Transubstantiation" (p. 66). Wever, however, uses the term in these lines in the sense that Jesus does with the Jews at Capernaum to refer to those who are unable to distinguish between the things of the flesh and the things of the spirit: "It is the Spirit that quickeneth; the flesh profiteth nothing; the wordes that I speake vnto you, are spirit and life" (John 6.63). Good Councell is condemning Juventus for indulging in his "fleshly swinish lustes" after he had promised that "suche fleshly fruites shuld not be sene" in him (l. 959). There is no inference that Juventus has returned to the faith of his elders (and thus presumably to a belief in transubstantiation), but rather that he has not followed God's word in his daily life, instead wallowing in the things of the flesh. If this use of the term "Capernite" is a veiled reference to the doctrine of transubstantiation, it is carefully presented in another, primary sense which would pass censorship under the Act of Six Articles.

Dramatic and Literary Qualities

That *Lusty Juventus* remained well known for a century after its composition is evident from the three sixteenth-century editions known to have been printed, from the borrowings in *The Booke of Sir Thomas Moore* (to be discussed later), and from references to the interlude in early seventeenth-century drama. In Ben Jonson's play *The Devil is an Ass,* the Vice character is said to be swearing like a "lusty Iuventus" (I. i. 44-53); and in *The Wise-woman Of Hogsdon,* Thomas Heywood, alluding to the romantic rather than the profane aspect of Wever's central character, has Taber thus address young Chartly (who enters "very gallant, in his hand a Lady"): *"Lusty Iuventus;* will it please you to draw neere," to which request the young man answers affirmatively and kisses the Lady.[1]

The dramatic and literary qualities that would account for this continued popularity are many, though the interlude has been scorned and neglected by nineteenth- and twentieth-century critics and editors.[2] In the first place, it is an amusing and dramatically well-constructed play as well as being morally and religiously enlightening — both teaching and delighting as all good Renaissance literature was supposed to do. The audience would be instructed by the good counsel and the many paraphrased biblical texts, and they would also be entertained by the lively songs, the witty dialogue, the revealing soliloquies, the disguise motif, a real devil on stage, and, above all, by the charmingly naïve but resilient young man Lusty Juventus and the clever con artist Hypocrisie. By actual line count, over half of the play consists of light entertainment — intrigue, satire, song, flirtation, and a young man living as "the course of nature doth him bind." The following outline will indicate Wever's dramatic artistry in the effective alternation of serious and comic scenes for contrasting effect:

Prologue	*serious*	36 lines	(Messenger)
Song	*light*	12 lines	(Juventus)
Soliloquy	*light*	21 lines	(Juventus)
Conversion	*serious*	254 lines	(Juventus, Good Councell, Knowledge)
Soliloquy	*light*	35 lines	(Deuyl)
Temptation Fall Life in Sin	*light*	525 lines	(Deuyl, Hypocrisie, Juventus, Felowshyp, and Abhominable Liuing)
Song	*light*	20 lines	(Juventus, Hypocrisie, Felowshyp, and Abhominable Liuing)
Soliloquy	*serious*	35 lines	(Good Councell)
Repentance	*serious*	145 lines	(Juventus — defiant, prostrate, despairing, repentant — Good Councell, and Gods Mercyfull Promyses)
Direct address to audience	*serious*	70 lines	(Juventus)
Prayer for king	*serious*	17 lines	(Good Councell and Juventus)
Total		1170 lines	(613 in light scenes).

The devil's soliloquy is here considered "light" even though he is very melancholy about his prospects of seducing mankind to follow his laws, because evil discomfited is comic to the intended victims — the audience.

Songs and soliloquies punctuate the more extended scenes of intrigue or good counsel; comic scenes alternate with serious scenes; and the stage fills (as much as four characters can fill a stage), empties to one actor, then fills to three for the final scene. The first song and soliloquy deftly characterize the pleasure-seeking young man, and other soliloquies are used to show the nature of the Deuyl and his clever son Hypocrisie and to point to ensuing action. Two soliloquies encapsulate the conversion scene — Juventus' before and the Deuyl's following — just as two soliloquies frame the temptation-fall scene — the Deuyl's preceding and Good Councell's lament coming directly after the gulling of Juventus.

The soliloquies also serve another purpose, allowing for costume changes so that, as the title page promises, "Foure [actors] may play it easely, takyng such partes as they thinke best: so that any one tak of those partes that be not in place at once." There are various possibilities for four actors doubling in the nine roles. For example if there were available two exceptionally good actors and two supporting ones, the following scheme for casting could be used:

Actor A — Juventus
Actor B — Good Councell and Hypocrisie
Actor C — Messenger, Deuyl, and Felowshyp
Actor D — Knowledge, Abhominable Liuing, and Gods Mercyfull Promyses

Having the same actor play both Good Councell and Hypocrisie (evil counsel) would add to the dramatic irony.

Another possibility, if three good actors were available along with one novice, would be the following:

Actor A — Juventus
Actor B — Knowledge (exiting at l. 321, changing costume during the Deuyl's soliloquy, and entering as Hypocrisie after l. 358) and Hypocrisie
Actor C — Good Councell and Felowshyp
Actor D — Messenger, Deuyl, Abhominable Liuing, and Gods Mercyfull Promyses

There are other possibilities, but the two parts requiring the best actors are those of Juventus, who is on stage most of the time, and Hypocrisie, the witty rogue, precursor of Aaron, Richard III, Iago, and Autolycus of Shakespeare's rogue's gallery. Hypocrisie's long satiric anti-clerical boast (ll. 378-443) about the superstitions he has foisted off on the world in the name of religion, while not a soliloquy, is a dramatic tour de force that would have brought the house down in a country recently freed from an overabundance of regular clergy and the unwelcome power of the Pope.

Though by using soliloquies and role limitations Wever has crafted the interlude to accommodate production by only four actors, there is one place that would necessitate an awkward costume change. At the end of the life-in-sin episode, the four characters — Hypocrisie, Juventus, Felowshyp, and Abhominable Liuing — move off stage singing, probably arm in arm in a kind of buck-and-wing exit (following l. 899), and Good Councell must enter for his soliloquy only four lines later (after l. 903). Obviously whichever actor was doubling for Good Councell would have had to be a quick-change artist, though possibly the music accompanying the song was extended to allow the actor to change his costume and re-enter as the serious good counsellor.

Wever's structural juxtaposing of scenes to achieve dramatic irony would also add to the audience's amusement. For instance, the entry of the Deuyl follows hard upon the exit of the overly confident young protagonist, who has rather easily been talked into an unnaturally religious frame of mind for one so young and lusty, and who has piously promised Good Councell and Knowledge,

>I wil neuer forsake your company,
>While 'I lyue in this world.
>
>(ll. 322-323)

The audience knows he is not likely to keep this innocent promise, and their recognition of his naïveté is reinforced by the immediate appearance on stage of the Deuyl, enemy of mankind, followed soon by his son Hypocrisie. Together these two discuss the effect of the conversion of youth, and Hypocrisie remains on stage, alone, to inform the audience just how he will seduce Juventus to live carnally by means of wicked company. Into this trap now wanders the recently converted young man, full of piety and good intent, carrying his gift New Testament, ripe for the inevitable fall. Hypocrisie greets him familiarly, vowing

>You are the last man,
>Which I talked on,
>I sware by thys day.
>
>(ll. 534-536)

Juventus is flattered, but the audience, of course, understands the comment in a different light.

Juventus is allured into the rogue's world by promise of a good time with the young girl Abhominable Liuing and Felowshyp. The four revelers exit with a lively song, and the irony of Juventus' broken promise is pointed up by the lone entry of a long-faced Good Councell lamenting the abominable living of his erstwhile convert and the general sin and vice rampant

DRAMATIC AND LITERARY QUALITIES

throughout the country. Wever's use of ironic contrast continues as the "new" worldly Juventus, on entering, mistakes the good fellow's words about the ungodly "Heaping sinne vpon sinne vice vpon vyce" (l. 937) for a dice game:

> Who is here playing at the Dice?
> I heard one speake of synnes and sice,
> His wordes did me entice,
> Hither to come.
>
> (ll. 939-942)

In addition to such careful structuring and use of scene contrast for ironic effect, Wever shows his artistry in his characterization in so short a space of the appealing teen-aged Juventus, whose first song illustrates a fancy lightly turned to thoughts of love:

> Therfore my hart is surely pyght,
> Of her alone to haue a sight
> Which is my ioy and hartes delyght,
> In youth is plesure, in youth is pleasure.
>
> (ll. 45-48)

Instead of the love he has dreamed of, he meets a sober Good Councell, surely a disappointment, and shows his independent spirit by asking penetrating questions of this intense, religious man before being converted to a promise of godly living. Neither is he an overly easy conquest when later Hypocrisie opens his campaign to gull him. Again Juventus requires some convincing, but since his heart was ready for love on his first entry, the girl Abhominable Liuing fans the dormant flames and Juventus is seduced. As Wever has succeeded in making him an appealing character in his innocence and fall, so he endears him to the audience in the sincerity of his prostration and utter despair. We are pleased with his repentance and are made willing to listen to his final personal appeal to the audience for reformation.

As to the costumes, one can only speculate since no costumes are described in Wever's play. It can be deduced, however, from the text that Deuyl is probably in a traditional devil costume since Hypocrisie immediately exclaims that the fellow is a salesman for the devil when he first catches sight of him:

> Sancti amen, who haue we there?
> By the masse I wil bie none of thy ware,
> Thou art a chapman for the deuell.
>
> (ll. 366-368)

Judging from stage directions in the medieval and early Tudor drama and from artists' conceptions of devils, the devil costume basically consisted of a black hairy animal suit with a monstrous horned headpiece, long claws on both feet and hands, and a tail culminating in a dart. Perhaps Wever's devil would not be costumed in full devil regalia, but he must certainly have had sufficient resemblance to the conventional stage devil to account for Hypocrisie's exclamation, "Sancti amen, . . . / Thou art a chapman for the deuell" (ll. 366-368).

How Hypocrisie is costumed cannot be determined from the text. Would he perhaps be dressed as a friar as is Bale's Hypocrisy in his *Three Laws* — or maybe as a "Popish doctor" as is the character False Doctrine from the same play? It is probable that he alters his dress before introducing himself to Juventus as a friend of his youth named Frendshyp, but he would have to make a quick change because the young man enters immediately after Hypocrisie's soliloquy. If he originally appeared as a friar, he could merely shed his clerical habit to become a layman as the Devil does in the medieval play *Wisdom Who is Christ* to become a gallant.

Juventus' dress also probably alters during the play, progressing from that of a carefree very young fellow, to a more prosperous young man who is accused by Hypocrisie of shunning his friends of leaner days, to a young gallant of the latest and most extreme fashion, a young blade who cuts and jags his clothes to suit his new life, much to the sorrow of Good Councell.

The costumes of the good counsel figures are not indicated, but perhaps consisted of academic robes of learned doctors. Nor is there any hint of the dress of Abhominable Liuing, though no problem would be encountered in showing her as a girl of free and easy morals, or of vnknowen honestie, as Hypocrisie addresses her (l. 789).

In addition to working out with great care and skill the structure and the dramatic aspects of *Lusty Juventus,* Wever shows an awareness of the traditional verse forms of the Tudor interludes by his use, for instance, of rhyme royal for his serious characters or the sextilla or six-line stanza (with tail rhyme) rhyming aabccb, for the longer speeches of his vice character Hypocrisie.[3] His meter is accentual with four and at times five heavy stresses to the line and a varying number of unstressed syllables to create short and long lines for Hypocrisie and long lines for the serious characters. He is not writing poetry but rather verse for a dramatic presentation; judged as such, his rhyming groups of lines are certainly adequate. They should not be analyzed for regularity in the individual lines, for, as J. E. Bernard has long ago pointed out, the individual line of verse

DRAMATIC AND LITERARY QUALITIES

was of little importance to the authors of Tudor interludes:

> That it [the line] should embrace now eight syllables, now thirty-eight, did not challenge their sense of form. The line was an atom and nothing more, and no account was taken of the fact that the atom might itself have strict form, that it might be composed of tinier particles charged with complexes of factual, rhythmic, or melodic association.[4]

Wever's lines never go to the extreme of having thirty-eight syllables, but they do vary considerably in length. Nor can it be said that Wever always thought of his lines as atoms having no internal structure; at times he very consciously structures lines by parallel forms, especially noticeable in the satiric boast given to Hypocrisie (ll. 408-443), and by the use of extensive internal rhyme in lines 1140-1153.

Other evidence of careful craftmanship in *Lusty Juventus* is to be found in Wever's interlocking rhyme scheme for the dialogue, resulting in a kind of comic echoing of sound from one speaker to the next: the last line of one character's speech rhymes with the first line of the next character's speech, as in the following interchange between Hypocrisie, Juventus, and Abhominable Liuing (emphasis added):

>   Hypocrisie:
>   Do not you loue Felowship and *me?*
>   Abhominable Liuing:
>   Ye by the masse I loue you al *thre,*
>   But yet in dede yf I should say the truth,
>   Amongest al other welcome Mayster *Youth.*
>   Juventus:
>   Ful greatly I do delight to kiss your pleasaunt *mouth*
>   I am not able your kyndnes to recompence,
>   I long to talke with you secretly, therfore let vs go *hence.*
>   Abhominable Liuing:
>   I agre to that, for I would not for .xx. *pence,*
>   That it were knowne where I haue *bene.*
>   Hypocrisie:
>   What and it were knowne it is no deadly *synne,*
>   As for my parte I do not greatly care,
>   So that they fynd not your proper buttockes bare.
>   (ll. 840-851)

Throughout the play this rhyming pattern is maintained, with some exceptions, even with the longer speeches.[5]

The two songs in the interlude are in four-line stanzas rhyming aaax, with the fourth line being a refrain repeated in all stanzas. The tunes for the songs are not indicated.

As was conventional in medieval and early Renaissance drama, Wever characterizes Juventus' profane stages by having him join in the swearing by all that is holy: "by God I sweare," "by Goddes grace," "by Gods foote," and most often "by the masse." But original is Wever's indication of the climax of the young man's fall into sin by an accumulation of oaths all of which relate to the mass. The height of his blasphemy, coming at the nadir of his seduction into carnal temptation by the girl Abhominable Liuing, is made emphatic by a concentration of oaths and vows which may be seen as representing an inversion of the sacrament of the eucharist:[6]

> By dogs precious woundes that was som whorson villain
> I wyll neuer eate meate that shal do me good,
> Tyl I haue cut his fleshe by gogs precyous blud,
> Tell me I praye who it was,
> And I wyl trim the knaue by the blessed masse.
> (ll. 804-808)

Suggested are Christ's sacrifice (l. 804), the proper receiving of the host in the sacrament (l. 805), the two elements of the sacrament (l. 806), and suggestions of violence paralleling the crucifixion of Christ (ll. 806, 808).

Adding further depth to the play, there is an allegorical level paralleling the literal story of a particular young man falling into and out of grace. Juventus, representing all English youth of the 1530's, is offered and accepts God's word in his own language, but the hoped-for universal virtue in all young people does not materialize; society is not reformed by this promised panacea, though Satan is worried that such may be the result. Through the world (loose friendship, gambling, and fine clothes) and the flesh (sexual license and natural appetite), the devil will undermine the good achieved by the new freedom to know the word of God. The allegorical moral: Satan is still at work in England and youth must be wary of his wiles, counteracting them by following God's commandments and remembering His merciful promises in the now-available scriptures. W. Roy Mackenzie finds difficulty with the allegory in Wever's interlude, especially with the character Hypocrisie, who, he concludes, "is best interpreted as representing a vice practiced by other people, through which the young man is deceived and led into a life of sin."[7] It seems obvious, however, that in the overall allegory of the play, representing the continuing battle between God and the envious Satan over God's new creation, man, Hypocrisie is a personification of the abstract quality of Satan's mind through which he presents evil as good to serve his purpose. Thus in the moral plays the vices always presented themselves disguised as virtues — hypocrisy at work.

Mackenzie also views too narrowly the character Good Councell as "the same sort of character as Hypocrisy the Vice," representing "either religious advice, or the people giving religious advice to Juventus,"[8] and Knowledge as representing "a virtue within the mind of the hero"; whereas actually both Good Councell and Knowledge are personifications of two abstract gifts of the Holy Spirit,[9] characters who, combined into the one character Knowledge, played a significant role in the medieval Catholic drama *Everyman*.[10] They are both examples of the many Wisdom figures who were sent by God to help illumine the path to virtue for fallen man. Included in these active divine agents were such characters as Grace Dieu in Lydgate's *The Pilgrimage of the Life of Man*, Dame Sapience in the *Court of Sapience*, and Celestial Sapience in Lydgate's *The Assembly of Gods*.

As we have seen, Wever's interlude is a tightly structured, elaborately worked-out piece of dramaturgy, worthy of being anthologized along with the inevitable *Everyman*, not only to demonstrate the treatment in the drama of the shift in the orthodox English religious position after 1534, but also to illustrate the artistic, literary, and dramatic value of the Tudor interludes.

Notes

[1] *The Dramatic Works of Thomas Heywood,* no editor given (1874; rpt. New York: Russell & Russell, 1964), Act 3, scene 1.

[2] In the nineteenth century, W. Carew Hazlitt's opinion of *Lusty Juventus* is typical: "This is certainly a piece of rather heavy and tedious morality, replete with good instruction, but didactic to a fault. It is deficient in the curious allusions, which abound in other productions of the same kind; and even that mysterious character *Abominable* [sic] *Living,* whose introduction promises some amusement and illustration, moves off the scene almost immediately after her first appearance, while *Little Bess,* whose entrance might have been a vehicle for some diverting or sentimental situation, does not 'come on' at all." *A Select Collection of Old English Plays* (1874-76; rpt. New York: Benjamin Blom, 1964), p. 44. And for the twentieth-century author W. Roy Mackenzie, the play "is remarkable chiefly for its astonishingly dull exposition of Scripture and its heaping up of Scriptural quotations, with careful reference to book and chapter" (p. 95);

he is confused by the allegory, which he finds not clear, and is generally annoyed by the play: "The least that one could ask in compensation for the dullness of the play is that the allegory should be unequivocal, but the author has made no concessions." *The English Moralities From the Point of Allegory* (Boston and London: Ginn, 1914), p. 98. David Bevington, *From Mankind to Marlowe: Growth of Structure in the Popular Drama of Tudor England* (Cambridge: Harvard Univ. Press, 1962), pp. 142-145, gives the play its due, praising its structure.

[3] According to J. E. Bernard, Jr., in *The Prosody of the Tudor Interlude* (New Haven: Yale Univ. Press, 1939), p. 207, the *rime couée* of the six-line stanza was the measure of the vices or lighter element in all of the Tudor interludes.

[4] Bernard, *Prosody*, p. 2.

[5] Bernard, *Prosody*, pp. 101-102, accuses Wever of leaving "Half a sixain couée . . . straggling on time and again." But these lines often made up the short-speech dialogue and so are justifiably truncated. Nor can we agree with Bernard's judgment that "From the prosodic point of view this drama is an *olla podrida* of slipshod versifying." Also his objection that many of Wever's rhymes are "monstrous," while justified in some cases, must be countered with the fact of changes in pronunciation over the centuries (as he admits) and the use of wrenched rhymes for comic effect as possibly in Shakespeare's Bottom rhyming "good" and "blood" in his death speech.

[6] I am indebted to a Catholic colleague, Samuel Southwell, for this suggestion.

[7] *The English Moralities*, p. 98.

[8] *The English Moralities*, p. 99.

[9] See Isaiah 11.1-3.

[10] See Helen S. Thomas, "The Meaning of the Character Knowlege in *Everyman*," *Mississippi Quarterly*, 14 (1960-61), 3-13.

Dramatic Context — Early Sixteenth Century

Earlier sections of this Introduction on the dating of Wever's interlude have sought to pinpoint the probable composition date as the last few years of the reign of Henry VIII, but *Lusty Juventus* should also be viewed in the broader context of the dramatic literature of the entire first half of the sixteenth century. In placing it in context, one must look at its relationship to the best known of all the moral plays, *Everyman*, which was repeatedly published in the first three decades of the century. The two plays are alike in being highly doctrinal and in showing the role of knowledge and good counsel in the salvation of the young protagonist, but the doctrine in *Everyman* is medieval Catholic, and in *Lusty Juventus,* as we have seen, late Henrician Protestant. The role of the good counsellor in *Everyman* is to point to the seven sacraments adminstered by the priesthood as the sacramental path to salvation, whereas in *Lusty Juventus* Knowledge and Good Councell preach Christ's Testament and God's Promises made to man as the "way," considering the scripture as its own interpreter.

Everyman is a play about the sacraments as means of strengthening man's good deeds and conveying spiritual blessings given no other way (the medieval thesis), whereas Wever's interlude, for whatever reason, avoids making any mention of the sacraments, except in the profanity. This omission may have been intended as a means of avoiding any censure that might have followed even the slightest deviation from the orthodoxy of the Act of Six Articles and especially any presentation of the sacraments as signs confirming and displaying God's eternal, unfailing promises, but as no more than signs and seals of the grace promised and claimed. Wever contented himself with presenting the need for gospel preaching, which, according to Reformation theology, holds forth audibly the same promises and the same Christ that the sacraments present visibly, and which calls for the same response of active approving faith.[1] But for the author of *Everyman,* it is the traditional seven "blessyd sacramentes," given out of Christ's "herte with grete pyne [suffering]," which infuse grace and constitute the path to man's redemption: the priest "bereth the keyes" and "byndeth and vnbyndeth all bandes, / Bothe in erthe and in heuen."[2]

The sacrament of Penance is acted out on stage in *Everyman:* confession is called "that clensynge ryuere" (l. 536) and is made to the holy priest Confession, who lives in "the hous of saluacyon" (l. 540). After Everyman has completed his penance, scourging his body as Christ was scourged, he will "wade the water clere" to save himself from purgatory, "that sharpe fyre" (ll. 617-618). The image of cleansing water is also used in *Lusty Juventus* but to refer to Christ's Testament, which is called "the well, or fountayne most clere, / Out of which doth spryng swete consolation, / To all those which thirst after eternal saluation" (ll. 280-282). Thus the preaching of the gospel brings the sweet consolation for Juventus that is obtained by Everyman through the sacrament of Penance. Juventus carries his gift New Testament as the Catholic priest did his portous, an abbreviated mass book, as a symbol of that part of religious ritual which is paramount in importance.

Before he will be ready to make a clear reckoning, Everyman will leave the stage to receive two additional sacraments off-stage — the sacraments of the Altar and of Extreme Unction. The author praises all seven of the "blessyd sacramentes" along with the priesthood, which is said to exceed "all other thynge" (l. 732), God having given more power to the priest than "to ony aungell that is in heuen" (l. 736):

> With v. wordes he may consecrate,
> Goddes body in flesshe and blode to make,
> And [he] handeleth his Maker bytwene his handes.
> (ll. 737-739)

The audience is informed that there is no remedy under God for salvation except priesthood, since

> . . . God gaue preest that dygnyte,
> And setteth them in his stede amonge vs to be;
> Thus be they aboue aungelles in degree.
> (ll. 747-749)

Such effusive praise of priests would hardly have been pleasing to Henry VIII after his break with Rome and his suppression of the religious houses in England. The Catholic *Everyman*, which had gone through many editions in the years from ca. 1500 to 1530, was not published again until the eighteenth century.[3]

A comparison and contrast of the two plays suggests the possibility of viewing *Lusty Juventus* as a direct reply by a reform cleric to the popular *Everyman* on the subject of salvation. Both plays take meaning from the biblical parable of the talents: *Everyman* by implication[4] and *Lusty Juventus* by direct reference (ll. 313-317). Both plays have similar good counsel figures: the character Knowledge in *Everyman* is split by Wever into Good Councell, Knowledge, and Gods Mercyfull Promyses, but the dramatic function is the same — to guide the sinful young man to salvation.[5] In *Lusty Juventus*, however, the "way" is through gospel preaching and Christ's Testament rather than the sacraments; the priesthood instead of being praised is criticized as "wicked teachers" of false doctrine to the ignorant elders of Juventus; the important role of Good Deeds in *Everyman* is significantly reduced in Wever's interlude to good deeds as signs of true faith; and Everyman's false friends and kinsmen are telescoped into the Vice character Hypocrisie, disguised as Frendshyp, and his boon companion Felowshyp. Although Juventus is not immediately faced with the prospect of giving an account of his life before the all-high judge as is Everyman, he anticipates the reckoning and warns the audience at the end of the play that they should not depend on friends and kinsmen to defend them at judgment day, thus naming the same people who had refused to accompany Everyman:

> Let not flatteryng Frendshyp, nor yet wicked company
> Perswade you in no wyse, Gods word to abuse
> But se that ye stand stedfastly vnto the viritie,
> And according to the rule therof, your doings frame & vse
> Neither Kinred nor Felowship shal you excuse,
> When you shal appere before the iudgement seat,
> But your own secret conscience shal then geue an audite.
> (ll. 1133-1139)

Although the two plays are alike in many ways, they contrast in the all-important way back after post-baptismal sin: Everyman confesses his sins to the priest and completes the sacrament of Penance, whereas Juventus confesses publicly to Good Councell and depends on penance the virtue rather than the sacrament (see above for a discussion of Henry VIII's position on penance as a virtue).

The point in Wever's play is that the miracle of a fundamentally inexplicable process of regeneration comes out of the word of God rather than out of ecclesiastical sacraments, ceremonies, and rules, many of which are incompatible with the gospel. He sees scripture as its own interpreter, following the Reformation principle that the Bible is interpreted by the Bible itself, and man can learn the will of God simply from His own literal word.[6]

Henry VIII's own position on this matter in the *King's Book* includes a semitraditional account of the seven sacraments but with great emphasis on his people knowing the *verbum dei* (given to them in their own tongue by his gracious majesty), relying on God's promises to man, and living according to the commandments found in God's word. On the whole, even with its omission of any mention of the sacraments, *Lusty Juventus* is infinitely more compatible with the *King's Book* than is the highly doctrinal *Everyman* in its panegyric on the priesthood and its exclusive emphasis on the sacraments controlled by the priesthood. Wever's play might well have been conceived as a conscious replacement for the Catholic *Everyman*. Whether so intended or not, it did in essence supplant the Catholic play, being printed and referred to throughout the sixteenth and into the seventeenth century.

Unlike *Everyman*, however, the anti-clerical and even anti-papal satire of another early sixteenth-century Catholic dramatist, John Heywood, found favor in the new climate of opposition to the usurped power of the Pope and the abuses of the religious houses in England. Heywood's interludes with their amusing Chaucerian satire of the greed and chicanery of pardoners and friars were more in tune with the times than the seriously doctrinal *Everyman*.

Heywood was even more pointed in his satire than was Wever. He substituted for Wever's generalized holy items ("Holy reliques" of Hypocrisie's "own inuencion" such as "Holy stockes" and "holy stones," "Holy cloughtes" and "holy bones" — ll. 439-440, 417-418) specific frauds in his satire of the Pardoner, who displays and touts the efficacy of such fantastic relics as the jaw-bone of All-Hallows, the great toe of the Trinity, the buttock-bone of Pentecost, the box of bees that stung Eve as she sat on her knees eating the forbidden fruit, the blessed arm of Saint Sunday, and the brain-pan of Saint Michael *(The Four PP,* printed 1533, and *The Pardoner and the Friar,* printed sometime between 1543 and 1547). As did *Lusty Juventus, The Four PP* remained popular throughout the century, being one of the several plays mentioned, along with *Lusty Juventus,* in *The Booke of Sir Thomas Moore* (see below for a discussion of the *Moore* play).

John Bale, as would be expected of the vocal Protestant reformer, goes beyond Wever and even Heywood in his irreverent invention of relics to be displayed by Stephen Langton, appointee of Pope Innocent II for Archbishop of Canterbury, in *King Johan,* probably written in the 1530's and revised some indeterminate time before Bale's death in 1563: "a bone of the blyssyd trynytye" and a "dram of þe tord of swete seynt Barnabe"; "a feddere of good seynt Myhelles wyng," and "a pece of Davyds harpe stryng"; a "lowse of seynt Fraunces," and a "scabe of saynt Iob"; a "nayle of Adams too [toe]," and a "maggott of Moyses with a fart of saynt fandigo."[7]

In *Lusty Juventus* Wever is working in this Chaucerian tradition of condemning false relics, but without Heywood's or Bale's ridiculous items. Ironically, Heywood, though a Pope-Catholic, managed to remain as court musician to Henry VIII,[8] while Bale fled to the continent and had his writings prohibited by the Royal Proclamation of 1546. Wever presumably escaped censure under Henry VIII, though he possibly may have been the Richard Wever named by Foxe as being among the priests and laymen examined at Lichfield under the reign of Queen Mary (see above).

Another well-known tradition in early sixteenth-century literature —

using a religious book as a symbolic hand-prop — is to be found in Wever's interlude. Juventus is given a New Testament by Good Councell just as Erasmus, in his colloquy "Cyclops, or the Gospel Bearer," had given his swaggering soldier Polyphemus a New Testament (as translated into Latin by Erasmus) painted saffron and bright red and blue.[9] It was a soldierly book "protected by bosses, plates, and brass clasps," which the hard-drinking soldier used to punish a "certain Franciscan" in his neighborhood who "kept babbling from the pulpit against Erasmus' New Testament." Erasmus, of course, is satirizing the New Gospellers, who ostentatiously carry the New Testament but do not live according to its precepts, by making Polyphemus use his Gospel to beat virtue into his opponents:

> I met the man privately, grabbed him by the hair with my left hand, and punched him with my left hand, and punched him with my right. I gave him a hell of a beating; made his whole face swell. What do you say to that? Isn't that promoting the gospel? Next I gave him absolution by banging him on the head three times with this very same book, raising three bumps, in the name of the Father, Son, and Holy Ghost (pp. 420-421).

Polyphemus' companion, Cannius, exclaims good-naturedly, "The evangelical spirit, all right! This is certainly defending the Gospel" (p. 421). The soldier confesses that he does not live chastely or keep God's commandments or do penance for his sins, but he does defend the gospel. Erasmus continues to have fun at the expense of the New Gospellers by showing the unchristian actions of Polyphemus as the burly soldier admits that he is not yet a "perfect follower of the gospel: just an ordinary fellow," his kind having "four gospels" of sensuality, which

> above all we gospellers seek: full bellies; plenty of work for the organs below the belly; a livelihood from somewhere or other; finally, freedom to do as we like. If we get these, we shout in our cups, "Io, triumphe; Io, Paean! The gospel flourishes! Christ reigns!" (p. 421).

In a less violent manner, Juventus the New Gospeller misuses his New Testament as an outward sign prominently displayed to ward off criticism of his sensual living with Frendshyp, Felowshyp, and Abhominable Liuing (ll. 687-691). Whether Wever knew Erasmus' dialogue is uncertain, but the parallel condemnation of the hypocritical use of the New Testament by two New Gospellers is suggestive,[10] and certainly the moral for both Wever and Erasmus is that following the teachings of the New Testament is the important part of Christianity.

By the use of sacred books on stage, symbolic significance was immediately and efficiently projected. For example, in the Latin play *Acolastus* by Gulielmus Gnapheus, first published in 1529, the young prodigal son is given a book — the *bibliorum codex,* a "set of moral precepts" — by which he is to regulate his conduct and to know when he has fallen into sin. At the hostility of his friend Philautus (self-love) towards the book, he throws it away, choosing to follow his own pleasures. There is some question whether the book is the whole Bible or just the Law as distinct from the Gospel, since it is referred to in the final act of the play as the *sacrum volumen legis.* [11] But since the Law would be included in the Bible, it seems likely that it was the Bible given to the young man. Gnapheus, the author, often accused of sympathy with the Reformation movement and twice imprisoned by the Inquisition,[12] maintains in the Prologue that "there is not a suspicion of new doctrine" in the play (p. 91). But by choosing the well-known parable of the prodigal son from the Gospel, and presenting it in the form of a play "within which is wrapped a mystery," he is able to suggest the religious new learning approach while avoiding forbidden doctrine. In his Epilogue he reminds the audience that God's Promises are to be trusted, a Reformation emphasis as is his oblique reference to the depravity of man: Christ employed the parable of the prodigal son to this end "that the more we grieve at being in conflict with God and born the children of wrath, the more we may rejoice at being restored to our Father's favour through the gift of the Holy Spirit . . ." (p. 203). Gnapheus is walking a tight rope with more caution than Wever was obliged to practice.

It is possible that Wever knew this popular biblical drama when he, like Gnapheus, used a sacred book as a symbolic hand property in *Lusty Juventus,* since *Acolastus* was translated into English in 1540. There is some similarity in Gnapheus' comment to the audience in the Prologue, "But I hear whispering among you, something about 'modern impudence' and 'teaching one's grandmother'" (p. 91), and Hypocrisie's sarcastic comment to Juventus:

> Wylt thou set men to scoole,
> When they be olde?
> . . . .
> The world was neuer mery,
> Since children were so bolde:
> Now euery boy wyl be a teacher
> The father a foole, and the chyld a preacher,
> This is preaty geare

DRAMATIC CONTEXT—EARLY SIXTEENTH CENTURY   lv

>   The foule presumption of youth
>   Wyl turne shortly to great ruth
>   I fere, I feare, I feare.
>   (ll. 648-649, 651-658)

John Bale also used the New Testament as a stage hand-prop in his play called *A Comedy Concernynge thre lawes, of Nature, Moses, & Christ, corrupted by the Sodomytes, Pharysees and Papystes*.[13] At the end of Act I, Deus Pater presents Christi Lex with a New Testament which he must use to instruct men:

>   Take this precious book for a token evident,
>   A seal of my covenant, and a living testament:
>   *Hic pro signo dat ei novum testamentum* —
>   They that believe it shall live for evermore,
>   And they that do not will rue their folly sore.
>   (p. 8)

Wever most likely would have been familiar with Bale's play ("compiled" in 1538) and his use of the continuing dramatic tradition of a symbolic sacred book on stage.

John Foxe, the martyrologist, also uses Christ's Testament as a symbolic property in his Latin play *Christus Triumphans*,[14] wherein the character Psyche, attacked by Satan in the underworld, is instructed by Christ to smite her enemy with the book he gives her. Satan is bruised and beaten with the book, to signify the victory of Christ over Satan. Although Foxe's play was published in Basel in 1556, there may have been an earlier edition in London in 1551, and T. W. Baldwin thinks the play may even have been written by Foxe in his university period at Oxford, 1539-1545.[15] Such an early dating for the composition of *Christus Triumphans* would point to a significant parallel with Wever's *Lusty Juventus*. Foxe's Satan has a sergeant named Psychephonus, literally "soul-killer," who is disguised as Hypocrisis under the cloak of a Franciscan friar. This pair are reminiscent of Wever's Satan and his son Hypocrisie, but Foxe's scatological satire is fiercer and more virulent than Wever's, as, for example, when he has the messenger of Hell tell the Pope, Pseudamnus, that he is losing the battle for the souls of the people:

>   Everywhere they're farting at your orders and shitting on your bulls.
>   Your keys are worthless, and your thunder and triple crown are
>   universally scorned, for they say Christ himself lives and that a body
>   which sustains two heads is a monstrosity. They say your pomp,
>   extravagance, lust, savagery, doctrine, poisonings, crimes, trickeries

and trumperies, and the tumult of their tragic life easily prove who you are: they firmly believe that you are the Antichrist . . . (p. 351). Both Foxe and Wever use Christ's Testament as a symbolic stage prop, but Wever's mild satire of the papists pales before such attacks as Foxe's.

Placing *Lusty Juventus* thus in the dramatic context of the early sixteenth century lends support to the earlier thesis argued in this Introduction that Wever's play not only could have been written during Henry VIII's period of religious retrenchment, 1540-1547, but that it better fits in that period than in the less restrained years of the Reformation in England: either before 1540 or between 1547 and the death of Edward VI in 1553.

Notes

[1] J. I. Packer, Introd., *The Work of Thomas Cranmer*, ed. G. E. Duffield (Philadelphia: Fortress, 1965), p. xv. It has been suggested by one of my colleagues that the oaths used by Juventus and other characters constitute references to the sacraments, but such oaths as "by the mass," "by God's blood," or "by God's bones" in the mouths of fallen characters were so common in medieval and Renaissance drama that little significance can be attributed to Wever's use of them.

[2] *Everyman*, ed. A. C. Cawley (Manchester, Eng.: Manchester Univ. Press, 1961), ll. 716, 720, 740-741. All further quotations from *Everyman* are taken from this text.

[3] W. W. Greg, *A Bibliography of the English Printed Drama* . . . I (London: for the Bibliographical Society, 1939), estimates that since the four surviving copies of *Everyman* are from different editions, there were probably at least ten editions of the play before 1530. Hawkins included the play in his *Origin of the English Drama*, 1773.

[4] V. A. Kolve demonstrates that the parable is the text behind *Everyman* in his essay "*Everyman* and the Parable of the Talents," in *The Medieval Drama*, ed. Sandro Sticca (Albany: State Univ. of New York Press, 1972), pp. 69-95. Although the text of the Parable of the Talents is not directly mentioned in *Everyman*, Kolve describes it as being "like the soil beneath a rich carpet of green grass: it has a great deal to do with everything we do see that is substantial, pleasing, and alive" in the play (p. 94).

[5] For the nature of the character Knowledge in *Everyman*, see Helen S. Thomas, "The Meaning of the Character Knowledge in *Everyman*," *Mississippi Quarterly*, 14 (1960-61), 3-13. In the medieval treatises on the vices and virtues, the ability to receive good counsel was defined as a gift of the Holy Spirit, and good counsel and knowledge were but different

aspects of Wisdom.

⁶The phrasing of the Reformation position on the scriptures in this paragraph is borrowed from Gottfried W. Locher, "Zwingli and Erasmus," in *Erasmus in English,* A Newsletter published by University of Toronto Press, No. 10 (1979-80), pp. 6, 7, and 8.

⁷*King Johan,* ed. Barry B. Adams (San Marino, Cal.: The Huntington Library, 1969), Act II, ll. 1215-1222. The play remained in manuscript until the 19th century. Bale also has Infidelitas present a powerful relic — "a wing of the Holy Ghost" — to save men from thunder and evil spirits in *Thre Lawes, The Dramatic Writings of John Bale, Bishop of Ossory,* ed. John S. Farmer (1907; rpt. New York: Barnes and Noble, 1966), Act IV, p. 64.

⁸He was forced to recant after being involved in the 1543 accusations against Cranmer and to confess his error in a treasonous plot to deprive King Henry VIII "of his royal dignity, title and name of 'Supreme Head of the English and Irish Church' . . ." but he was returned to royal favor and his lands and annuities restored. An account of his recantation is given in Robert W. Bolwell, *The Life and Works of John Heywood* (New York: Columbia Univ. Press, 1921), pp. 38-40.

⁹*The Colloquies of Erasmus,* trans. Craig R. Thompson (Chicago and London: Univ. of Chicago Press, 1965). All further references to this work appear in the text.

¹⁰The New Testament continued to be used as a symbol for good in W. Wager's 1569 play *The Longer Thou Livest the More Fool Thou Art,* ed. R. Mark Benbow, Regents Renaissance Drama Series (Lincoln, Nebraska: Univ. of Nebraska Press, 1967). It is contrasted with a deck of cards, which are symbolic of the sinful life. The good counsellor Piety gives Moros a Testament, "Wherein you shall learn what the will of God is," but the Fool is disappointed that there are no saints pictured in it as in the Catholic Primers and Hours of the Virgin Mary. He is more delighted with a pack of cards given him by the Vice character Idleness since this "book" has of "saints a great sort":

> Gods, see here is a goodly gentlewoman,
> Here are specks — some black, some red as blood.
> Teach me this book, I pray you, perfectly to con.
> (ll. 783-785)

The Vices instruct him to cast away the Testament and learn from the new book; being a fool, he will follow their advice.

Edmund Spenser, though not a dramatist, will later in the century work

in this tradition when he has Redcrosse Knight give Prince Arthur a New Testament:
> A booke, wherein his Saveours testament
> Was writ with golden letters rich and brave;
> A worke of wondrous grace, and able souls to save.
>   *(FQ,* I. ix. 19)

and when he makes Fidelia (Faith) carry a New Testament:
> A booke, that was both signed and seald with blood,
> Wherein darke things were writ, hard to be understood.
>   *(FQ,* I. x. 13)

Fidelia teaches "her sacred Booke, with bloud ywrit, / That none could read, except she did them teach." *(FQ,* I. x. 19).

[11]*Acolastus, A Latin Play of the Sixteenth Century* by Gulielmus Gnapheus, ed. W. E. D. Atkinson (London and Ontario, Canada: Univ. of Western Ontario, 1964), p. 58. First published in 1529, the play became a best seller, being reprinted eleven times within five years in Antwerp, Paris, Cologne, Leipzig, and Basel. In English the earliest known translation is by John Palgrave, 1540. All further references to this work appear in the text.

[12]Atkinson, *Acolastus,* Introduction, p. 1.

[13]*The Dramatic Writings of John Bale,* ed. Farmer, Act I, p. 8.

[14]John Foxe, *Christus Triumphans,* in *Two Latin Comedies by John Foxe The Martyrologist,* trans. and ed. John Hazel Smith (Ithaca and London: Cornell Univ. Press, 1973).

[15]Cited by Smith, *Christus Triumphans,* p. 31.

Lusty Juventus, The Booke of Sir Thomas Moore, and Shakespeare

Lusty Juventus gains importance from its possible association with Shakespeare, who it is believed wrote in his own hand some of the scenes in the fragmentary and multi-authored manuscript *Booke of Sir Thomas Moore,*[1] a play which includes a scene and some lines borrowed from *Lusty Juventus.* In the *Moore* play, Sir Thomas More, for the entertainment of his banquet guests, is offered his choice of several plays, among which are *Lusty Juventus* and *The Marriage of Wit and Wisdom,* and although he ostensibly chooses the latter, the scene and lines actually played are from *Lusty Juventus* (ll. 37-48; 767-803; and 811-815). When one actor turns out to be missing, having gone to fetch a beard, Sir Thomas steps in and improvises the role of Good Councell. The performance is interrupted when he is called to court and the players are paid off, resulting in some grumbling on their part. The choice of this play and this role for Sir Thomas More, the ardent and learned Catholic layman who had defended the faith against William Tyndale, is certainly ironic since he and Good Councell would undoubtedly have given diametrically opposite counsel if the play had been performed in full and he had been able to finish his impromptu part. If the choice of the interlude for More lay in the hands of the dramatist Anthony Munday, who is given credit for authorship of much of the fragmentary play, the jest may well have been intentional since Munday's sympathies lay with the Reformation cause.

As J. M. Nosworthy points out, the borrowed passages are changed somewhat to fit different characters — for example, Juventus' lines are given to Wit, Hypocrisie's to Inclination, and those of Abhominable Liuing to Lady Vanitie.[2] Many of the changes in phrasing are insignificant, but Nosworthy suggests that some changes "anticipate those later imposed on drama by the Act of Abuses" and "argue that the adapter was not merely anti-Romanist but also decidedly Puritan in outlook," a description which fits Anthony Munday. The changes, omitting certain oaths, are quoted by Nosworthy as follows (Nosworthy's line numbers):

L.J. 794:   You shal not go yet by god I sweare,
S.T.M. 1086:   you shall not be gon as yet I sweare.
L.J. 803:   Yes by the masse that I would,
S.T.M. 1097:   yes in good sadnesse Lady, that I would.
                                                (p. xxiii)

The softened oaths in the *Moore* play take away some of the special character of Wever's Juventus, who was known in the early seventeenth century for his swearing as shown by Ben Jonson's Vice character swearing like a "lusty Iuventus" in *The Devil is an Ass* (I. i. 44-53).

Another variation in material borrowed into the *Moore* play — the expansion of an incomplete line — is pointed out as important by Nosworthy:

L.J. 793:   What vnknowen honestie a worde
S.T.M. 1085:   what, vnknowne honestie, a woord in your eare.

Nosworthy judges this addition significant because it furnishes an "eminently judicious" rhyme for "sweare" in line 794 and "here" in line 796

(Nosworthy's line numbers) and completes what seems to be a defective line in the sixteenth-century quartos of *Lusty Juventus,* but there is difficulty, he says, "in deciding whether or not it is authoritative" (p. xxiv). Arguing against its authoritativeness, it should be pointed out, is the special rhyming characteristic of Wever's interlude (discussed above) in which the last line of one character's speech is rhymed with the first line of the next character's speech. This interlocking rhyme scheme makes it more likely that the defective line (l. 789 in the present text) should read, "What vnknowen honestie a worde I pray," to pick up the rhyme of the last line of the preceding speech, "Come Felowship come on a waye" (l. 788), and that of line 791, "Here is none but your frindes, you nede not to fraie." Whoever supplied the phrase "a woord in your eare" to Wever's line 789 (the present text) for the *Moore* play, showed himself unaware of the curious interlocking rhyme scheme of Wever's interlude.

There is good evidence that Shakespeare had a hand in *Sir Thomas Moore.* The borrowings from *Lusty Juventus* are not located in the section that Shakespeare is thought to have written, but he doubtless knew the whole play, and thus would at least have been aware of Wever's Morality, even if he had not read it. None of the claims for actual borrowing from *Lusty Juventus* by Shakespeare is convincing,[3] but William H. Matchett's discussion is worth taking into account. He points out a verbal similarity with *Othello,* an image cluster, in the section of the *Moore* fragment written in Hand D (presumably Shakespeare's handwriting) in which the accusation "You would have us upon th'hip" in the *Moore* fragment parallels Iago's phrase "I'll have our Michael Cassio on the hip" in Shakespeare's *Othello.*[4]

Since Iago is widely recognized to owe much to the traditional Vice figure, a comparison of Shakespeare's villain with the Vice figure in the play he certainly knew of and may well have read is to the point. The date of the *Moore* play is a matter of debate among scholars, but most place it around 1600 or 1601, not long before the writing of *Othello* (probably 1602). From such a tenuous linking, one can conclude with certainty only that there might have been some influence from *Lusty Juventus* to *Othello.* Wever's interlude has the structure of the morality play as does Shakespeare's *Othello.* There is also a striking similarity between Wever's Vice character Hypocrisie and Shakespeare's Iago, as Bernard Spivack points out.[5] Like Iago, Hypocrisie questions himself in a soliloquy about his plans for revenge. "How shall I bring this geare to passe?" he asks, and then after a pause answers himself, "I can tell now bye the masse, / . . . I wyl infect hym with wicked company . . ." (ll. 495, 496-498). And again like Iago, Hypocrisie is pleased with his own cleverness: "Thus will I conuey, / My matter I say / Somewhat hansomely" (ll. 519-521).

Other similarities can be cited. As with Iago, the basis of Hypocrisie's success is his professing of love for the man he is duping ("By the masse I loue you so hartely, / That there is none so welcome to my cumpany," ll. 580-581), and masking himself under the guise of Frendshyp. Iago uses this same love-friendship avowal in the parallel seduction of not only Othello but also Roderigo and Cassio. Hypocrisie assures Juventus, "And if I did not loue you as nature doth me bynde, / You should not know so muche of my mynde" (ll. 637-638); Othello would know what is in Iago's mind: "By heauen I'le know thy Thoughts" (Q 1), but Iago answers, "You cannot," though finally because of his "Loue" for Othello, he will be frank: "For now I shall haue reason / To shew the Loue and Duty that I beare you / With franker spirit" (III. iii. 189-190, 222-224).[6]

The similarities continue. Like Iago, Hypocrisie is crude in his sexual jests and ironic in his commentary on his dupes. Both are in themselves good actors and clever in teaching the art of hypocrisy to their gulls: Hypocrisie shows Juventus how to play the actor, how to be a hypocrite so that he can live a lustful life without being challenged by the preachers (ll. 679-690), and Iago instructs Roderigo and Othello how to act their parts in achieving their goals — Roderigo's to enjoy Desdemona and Othello's to discover Desdemona's infidelity. Hypocrisie boasts of using the girl for his "purse":

> Then you shal se my cunnyng.
> . . . .
> The kynde heart of hyrs,
> Hath eased my purse,
> Many a time ere this.
> (ll. 711, 714-716)

Iago boasts that he "euer" makes "my Foole [Roderigo], my purse" (I. iii. 407). Both Hypocrisie and Iago receive the thanks of their victims for being made fools: Juventus thanks Hypocrisie for seducing him into a sinful life, "And I thanke you hertely for your kindnes" (l. 745); Iago is delighted with his plan to gull Othello and receive thanks for it, "I'le . . . / Make the Moore thanke me, loue me, and reward me / For making him egregiously an Asse" (II. i. 338, 341-342). Hypocrisie accuses Juventus of having too much religion; Iago says to Cassio, "You are too seuere a Moraller" (II. ii. 327). Such parallels tantalizingly point to the possibility of direct influence.

Both Hypocrisie and Iago are Vice characters in having the active role of intriguer and deceiver, though Irving Ribner suggests that Iago is really a Devil figure rather than a Vice. Leah Scragg pursues this idea, rightly pointing out numerous Devils in the early Mystery Cycles and morality plays, as well as in the drama of the sixteenth century, who have characteristics akin to those of Iago.[7] She concludes that "the Devil's claim to be Iago's forefather is at least as good as that of the Vice, and is supported by evidence in the play" (p. 64). Her chief concern seems to be to refute the contention that Iago is a motiveless, amoral character, "an amoral survivor from the psychomachia, roughly clad in the garments of realism . . ." (p. 64). That Iago is "related to the powers of darkness," as she asserts (p. 61), is certainly true, but the Vice character was also related to these powers, being both dramatically and theologically the son of the Devil. Wever's Hypocrisie is actually introduced by his father, the Deuyl, who reminds him, "I am thine owne father Sathan" (l. 371). Nor is the Vice character necessarily amoral. Hypocrisie, for example, though motivated by fear of his father, also passes moral judgment on his own activities undertaken on his father's behalf:

> I haue bene busyed, since the world began,
> To graffe thy lawes in the heart of man,
> Where they ought to be refused:
> And I haue so mingled Gods commaundementes,
> Wyth vaine zeales, and blynd ententes,
> That they be greatly abused.
>
> *(Lusty Juventus,* ll. 396-401)

Shakespeare does not distinguish clearly between the Devil figure and the Vice character. Both being related to the powers of darkness, it is probable that Iago has elements of both character types — father and son.

Whether Shakespeare knew Wever's *Lusty Juventus* we cannot say for sure, but his part in the compilation of the *Moore* play and the similarities provisionally suggested here point to the conclusion that he did.

Notes

[1] The possibility of Shakespeare's having written three pages of *The Booke of Sir Thomas Moore* was first suggested in 1871 by Richard Simpson, who felt that the play's imagery and style were Shakespearean; see "Are There Any Extant MSS. in Shakespeare's Handwriting?" *Notes & Queries,* 4th S, 8 (1871), 1-3. Since that early hint, literary scholars have concluded that Hand D in the manuscript is, indeed, Shakespeare's, and

that there is in addition orthographical and bibliographical as well as literary evidence based on style, imagery, and thought for Shakespeare's authorship of some scenes in *Sir Thomas Moore;* see *Shakespeare's Hand in The Play of Sir Thomas More: Papers by Alfred W. Pollard, W.W. Greg, E. Maunde Thompson, J. Dover Wilson, and R.W. Chambers . . .*, ed. W. W. Greg (Cambridge: Univ. Press, 1923). Although there is still some opposition to this conclusion, Samuel Schoenbaum thinks that the "support for the thesis of Pollard and company has been overwhelming"; see *Internal Evidence and Elizabethan Dramatic Authorship: An Essay in Literary History and Method* (Evanston: Northwestern Univ. Press, 1966), p. 107. More recently Schoenbaum writes that "a broad spectrum of evidence supports the Shakespeare attribution" and that scholarly opinion "now also favors ascription to Shakespeare of a shorter addition, a twenty-one-line speech by Moore, which is, however, in the hand of a professional playhouse scribe"; see *William Shakespeare: A Compact Documentary Life* (New York: Oxford Univ. Press, 1977), p. 215 and n., p. 217.

²Introd. *Lusty Juventus* (Oxford: for the Malone Society, 1971). All further references to Nosworthy are in the text.

³Thomas Hawkins, the eighteenth-century editor of *Lusty Juventus,* calls attention to some similarities of phrasing in Wever's interlude and in Shakespeare's plays: when Hypocrisie is attempting to persuade Juventus to abandon his idea of going to a "*preaching,*" he says that the preacher will not tell him anything new —

>Tush, what he will say I know ryght well:
>He wyll say that God is a good man,
>He can make him no better, and say the best he can.
>(ll. 600-602)

Shakespeare puts the words "God's a good man" into the mouth of Dogberry in *Much Ado About Nothing* (III. v. 39), "with great humour," says Hawkins. He also sees a similarity in Shakespeare's phrasing, "I shall desire you of more acquaintance" in the address of Bottom to Master Cobweb in *A Midsummer Night's Dream* (III. i. 188), and a locution used by Felowshyp when he says to Juventus, "I shal desyre you of better acquaintaunce" (l. 739). Hawkins finds that the spelling of Wever's character Abhominable Liuing helps unravel a verbal jest in *Love's Labor's Lost* when the pedant Holofernes laments the slovenly habit of speech of Don Armado, who would pronounce "abhominable" as "abbominable" (V. i. 27-28). *The Origin of the English Drama . . .* (Oxford: Clarendon, 1773), Vol. I, pp. 141, 146, 138.

⁴"Shylock, Iago, and Sir Thomas More: With Some Further Discussion of Shakespeare's Imagination," *PMLA,* 92 (1977), 219-220. Matchett also calls attention to the use of a similar phrase by Shylock in *The Merchant of Venice.*

⁵This similarity is discussed briefly by Spivack in *Shakespeare and the Allegory of Evil* (New York: Columbia Univ. Press, 1958), pp. 153, 167. He also finds similar parallels between Iago and other Vice characters, but there is no direct evidence linking Shakespeare with these other plays, whereas he certainly could have used Wever's Vice, Hypocrisie, as a model for Iago because of his involvement with the *Moore* play.

⁶*A New Variorum Edition of Shakespeare,* ed. Horace Howard Furness (1886; rpt. New York: Dover, 1963). All further references to *Othello* are in the text.

⁷Irving Ribner, *Patterns in Shakespearean Tragedy* (London: Methuen, 1960), p. 95; and Leah Scragg, "Iago — Vice or Devil?" *Shakespeare Survey,* 21 (1968), 53-65. All further references to this latter work are in the text.

Notes on the Present Text

The present text is based on a collation of the three known sixteenth-century editions of *Lusty Juventus:* the Vele edition in the Bodleian Library, the Copland and the Awdely copies in the British Library, and films of the Huntington Library copies of the Copland and Awdely editions, and of the Pforzheimer Library copy of the Copland edition.

Although the present text is based on the Vele edition in wording, I have attempted to make it physically resemble the Awdely quarto, which is by far the most readable of the three sixteenth-century texts. The character tags (speech prefixes) and stage directions in the Vele and Copland quartos are crowded into the margins (right-hand margin on the recto pages and left-hand on the verso pages), making the solid block of text on the page not only unattractive but also difficult to read and connect with the right character. As a result of this economical format, the text is compressed into five gatherings ([A.i.]-[E.ii.ᵛ] Vele; [A.i.]-[E.iii.] Copland) as compared with the somewhat more extensive Awdely text ([A.i.]-[F.ii.]), with its character tags and stage directions centered between the lines.

All three texts are in blackletter type, Vele and Copland using smaller black letter for stage directions, and Awdely only for the subtitle on the title page; none makes any use of italic or roman type. Awdely employs the paragraph sign frequently: (1) on the title page— preceding the title, the names of the players, and the instructions for doubling; (2) on [A.i.^{v}] — preceding the Prologue and each paragraph thereof; and (3) throughout the text — preceding each character tag and stage direction. Copland and Vele use the sign sparingly: Vele once on the title page, and Vele and Copland to precede the Prologue, each paragraph in the first one and one half pages, and the first stage direction. Vele uses, for no apparent reason, a double paragraph sign, one reversed facing the other, in the right-hand margin on sigs. [B.iii.^{v}], [B.iiii.^{v}], C.i., [C.iii.^{v}], and [D.i.^{v}]; two paragraph signs are preceded by a fist (finger extended, pointing to each), sigs. [B.iii.^{v}] and [B.iiii.^{v}].

The three quartos are in good condition and complete except for the Vele edition quarto, which has two torn leaves: the bottom right corner of sig. [B.iii.] and the top left corner of sig. E.ii. have been torn away, resulting in lines 403-409, 436, 1126-1128, 1160-1162 partially missing, and lines 437-443 entirely missing. The two leaves have been invisibly mended. In the left margin of sig. [E.i.^{v}] of the Awdely quarto copy in the British Library, there is written in black ink, in large handwriting, "Don Quixot's Wind = mil's" and several illegible letters, all underlined in a jagged black line.

Further evidence that the three sixteenth-century editions were printed as inexpensively as possible can be seen in the considerable number of errors in the printing of the signatures. The Vele text leads in the number of careless irregularities: punctuation in the signatures, omission of signatures, and faulty capitalization. Copland's and Awdely's editions have fewer of these mistakes, with Awdely's text being superior yet again to the other two in accuracy as well as in appearance.

All three texts, though for the most part unornamented, have the following ornaments: on the title page, a small leaf ornament in Copland (see McKerrow, *Title-page Borders,* No. 28, for five such leaf ornaments) and a small stylized ornament in Vele to precede the title; a truncated pyramid or trapezoid consisting of eight stylized ornaments like that preceding the title in Vele, to finish out the title page in Awdely; a very large capital F and I to begin the Prologue and the Song, the I in Vele being enclosed in an abstractly ornamented ruled square. On the colophon page, in Vele there are almost-text-wide historiated ornaments, and in Awdely almost-text-wide scroll side pieces printed horizontally above and below the colophon, in addition to a large truncated pyramid or trapezoid built of twenty-seven of the small stylized ornaments found on the title page; in Copland there is an almost-text-wide geometric ornament, which resembles an inverted printer's head piece, following the colophon.

None of the ornaments are to found in McKerrow, with the exception of the small leaf preceding the title in the Copland edition, which is repeated to form the right side border in *Printers'*, No. 73 and *Title-page Borders*, No. 28.[1] The Vele ornaments on the colophon page are the most elaborate: the upper one shows the figure of a fool blowing a long trumpet, with scrolls and an apparent devil head at the botton of a narrow side piece printed horizontally; the lower one is over three times as thick as the upper and contains a rose and vine leaves pattern, the rose resembling the one used by Robert and William Copland in their rose and garland device (McKerrow *Printers'*, Nos. 71-a and 71-b), but the leaves being quite different from those in the Copland device.

Punctuation: the punctuation is essentially that of the Vele edition, with the exception of corrections of obvious printer's errors and some "selective modernization"[2] for clarification of the text. All changes in punctuation, whether my own insertions or substitutions from the Copland or Awdely texts, have been indicated in the textual notes.

Spelling: to avoid submerging the "lively and Protean variety"[3] of sixteenth-century spelling, I have retained the old spelling as it appears in the Vele edition with the exception of some corrections of obvious errors, the substitutions usually drawn from the Copland or Awdely texts and always indicated in the textual notes. The names of the characters in character tags have been regularized to the form given on the title page of the Vele quarto. Capitalization of proper names and of the initial letter at the beginning of each line has been regularized and the changes indicated in the textual notes. Contractions in the Vele text have been silently expanded (for example, thē to them; fashiō to fashion; ẇdrawen to withdrawen; ẙ to the; ẙ to that) and indicated in the textual notes, where the superior letters have been indicated by regular letters, as wt, ye, and yt. Different forms of s have not been distinguished.

The extensive and apparently unsystematic differences in spelling in the three texts are noted only when they are substantive in nature, or incidentally in connection with the changes in punctuation of the Vele text.

Line numbering: line numbers are exclusive of stage directions, which are assigned the number of the immediately preceding line followed by a decimal point and 1 in the textual notes; for example, the stage direction following 1.69 is numbered 1.69.1.

Other changes:
- character tags and stage directions (abbreviated SD) have been centered between the speeches as in the Awdely edition instead of being crowded into the margins as in the Vele and Copland texts. The paragraph signs preceding the character tags and stage directions in Awdely and in the first forty-nine lines of the Vele and Copland texts have been omitted. A few stage directions have been added in brackets, when needed.
- emphasis has been added in the stage directions.
- catch words and signatures have been omitted.
- stanzas, rhyme royal or sextilla, have been set off with spaces to point up the regularity of the verse, and paragraph indention for the first line of stanzas or separate speeches has been regularized.

Notes

[1] Ronald B. McKerrow, *Printers' & Publishers' Devices in England and Scotland 1485-1640* (London: for the Bibliographical Society, 1913) and *Title-page Borders used in England & Scotland 1485-1640* (London: for the Bibliographical Society, 1932).

[2] G. B. Evans, "Shakespeare Restored — *Once Aain!*" in *Editing Renaissance Dramatic Texts: English, Italian, and Spanish,* ed. Anne Lancashire (New York and London: Garland, 1976), p. 49, suggests selective modernization to enable the text to retain "the fluidity and cohesiveness of the original without imposing on [it] as a whole either a merely antiquarian faithfulness or the Iron Maiden of modern logical punctuation."

[3] Evans' phrase, p. 48, "Shakespeare Restored . . ."

AN ENTERLUDE CALLED LUSTY IUUENTUS

An Enterlude called
Lusty Iuuentus.

Liuely describyng the frailtie of youth:
of nature, prone to vyce: by grace
and good councell trayn =
able to vertue.

The Personages that speake,
   Messenger.
   Lusty Iuuentus.
   Good Councell.
   Knowledge.
   Sathan the Deuyl.
   Hypocrisie.
   Felowshyp.
   Abhominable Liuing.
   Gods Mercyfull Promyses.

Foure may play it easely, takyng such par
tes as they thinke best: so that any one tak
of those partes that be not in place at once.

The Prologue of the messenger.
Gene. viii.
Iere. xvii.
Eccle. xxx.

For as much as man is naturally prone
To euil from hys youth, as scripture doth recite,
It is necessary, that he be spedyly withdrawen
From concupiscence of sin, hys naturall appetite,
5 In ordre to bring vp youth, Ecclesiasticus doth write,
An vntamed horse, wyll be harde sayth he,
And a wanton chylde, wylful wyll be.

Giue him no libertie in youth, nor hys folly excuse,
Bow downe his necke, and kepe him in good awe,
10 Leaste he be stubburne: no laboure refuse
To trayne hym to wisedome and teache him Gods law:
For youth is frayle and easy to drawe
By grace to goodnes: by nature to yll:
That nature hath ingrafted, is harde to kyll.

15   Neuertheles, in youth men maye be best
Trayned to vertue by godly mean,
Uice may be so mortified and so supprest,
That it shall not breake furth, yet the roote will remayn:
As in thys Enterlude by Youth, you shal se playn:
20 From his lust by Good Counsell, brought to godly conuersation
And shortly after to frayle natures inclination.

The enemy of mankynd, Sathan through Hipocrisy,
Fayned or chosen holines of mans blind entent,
Forsakyng Gods word, that leadeth the right way,
25 Is brought to Felowshyp and vngracyous company:
To Abhominable Liuing, till he be wholly bent

And so to desperation if Good Counsell were not sent
From God that in trouble doth no man forsake
That doth call and trust in hym for Christes sake.

30   Finally, Youth by Goddes special grace,
Doth earnestly repent his abhominable liuinge
By the doctrine of Good Councell, and to his solace,
Gods mercy entreth to him recitinge:
Gods mercifull promises, as they be in writinge,
35 He beleueth and foloweth, to his great consolacion.
All these partes ye shal se briefly played in their fashion.

Here entreth Lusty Iuuentus or, Youth singing as foloweth.

[Iuuentus.]
In a herber grene, a slepe where as I lay,
The byrdes sang swete in the middes of the day,
I dreamed fast of myrth and play.
40 In youth is plesure, in youth is pleasure.

Me thought I walked stil to and froo,
And from her company I could not go,
But when I waked it was not so,
In youth is plesure, in youth is plesure.

45   Therfore my hart is surely pyght,
Of her alone to haue a sight,
Which is my ioy and hartes delyght,
In youth is plesure, in youth is pleasure.   *Finis.*

Lusty Iuuentus or Youth he speaketh.

What how are they not here?

50 I am disapoynted by the blessed masse,
I had thought to haue found them making good chere
But now they are gone to some secret place.
Wel seing they are gone, I do not greatly passe.
Another time I wil hold them as much,
55 Seing they breake promise, and kepe not the touch.

What shal I do now to passe away the day?
Is there any man here that wil go to game?
At what soeuer he wyl play,
To make one, I am redy to the same:
60 Youth full of plesure is my proper name,
To be alone is not my appetie,
For of al thinges in the world I loue mery company.

Who knoweth where is ere a mynstrell?
By the masse I would fayne go daunce a fitte
65 My companions are at it I know right well
They do not al this whyle in a corner syt:
Agaynst another time they haue taught me wytte,
I beshrew theyr hartes for seruyng me thys,
I wyll go seke them, whether I hyt or mysse.

Here entreth Good Councell, To whom Youth yet speaketh.

70   Well I met father, well I met.
Dyd you heare anye mynstrels playe?
As you came hetherward vpon your waye,
And if you dyd I praye you wyse me thyther,
For I am going to seke them, & in fayth I know not whether.

Good Councell.

75   Syr I wyl aske you a question by your fauour,
What would you with the minstrell do?

Iuuentus.
Nothyng but haue a daunce or two,
To passe the tyme away in pleasure.

Good Councell.
If that be the matter I promyse you sure,
80 I am the more soryer that it shoulde so be,
For there is no such passing the time apointed in the scripture
Nor yet therunto it doth not agre.
I wyshe that ye would so vse your libertye,
To walke as you are bound to do,
85 Accordyng to the vocation whych God hath called you to.

Iuuentus.
Why syr, are you angry because I haue spoken so?
By the masse it is alone for my appety.

Good Councell.
Shewe me your name I praye you hertely.
And then I wyll my mynde expresse.

Iuuentus.
90   My name is called Iuuentus doutles,
Say what you wyll I wyll gyue you the hearinge.

Good Councell.
For as much as God hath created you of nothynge,
Unto hys owne lykenes by spiritual illumynacyon,
It is vnmete that ye should leade your liuynge,
95 Contrary to hys godly determynacyon.
Saint Paul vnto the Ephesians giueth good exhortacion
Saying, walke circumspectly, redemyng the tyme,
That is to spend it well, & not to wickednes encline.

Iuuentus.
No, no, hardely none of myne,
100 Yf I wold lyue so straight you myght counte me a foole.
Let them kepe those rules whych are doctours dyuine
And haue bene brought vp al theyr dayes in scole.

Good Councell.
Moyses in the lawe exhorteth hys people,
As in the boke of Deuteronomie he doth plainly write,
105 That they should liue obedient and thankefull,
For in effect these wordes he doth resite:
Al ye thys day stand before the lordes syght,
Both princes, rulers, elders and parentes,
Children, wiues, yong & old, therfore obey his
         commaundementes.

Iuuentus.
110 I am to yonge to vnderstand his documents,
Wherfore dyd al they stand before hys presence?

Good Councell.
To enter wyth God peace and alyaunce,
Promisinge that they woulde him honour feare & serue.
Al kynd of people were bound in those couenauntes,
115 That from hys lawe they shuld neuer swarue,
For God vseth no parcialitie.

Iuuentus.
What, am I bound as wel as the cleargy,
To learne and folow his preceptes and lawe?

Good Councell.
Yea surely, or els God will with drawe

120 His mercy from you promised in his couenaunt,
For except you liue vnder his obedience and awe,
How can you receiue the benefites of his testament?
For he that submitteth hym selfe to be a seruaunt,
And his maisters commaundement wil not fulfil nor regard,
125 Acording as he hath done, is worthy his reward.

Iuuentus.
It is as true a saying as euer I heard,
Therfore your name I pray you now tell,
For by my truth your communicacion I like wonders well.

Good Councell.
My name is called Good Councell.

Iuuentus.
130   Good Councell,
Now in fayth I cry you mercy,
I am sory that I haue you thus offended,
But I pray you beare wyth me paciently,
And my misse behauyour shal be amended,
135 I know my time I haue rudely spended,
Folowyng my owne lust being led by ignoraunce,
But nowe I hope of better knowlege through your
                                    acquaintaunce.

Good Councell.
I pray God guide you with his gracious assistans,
Unto the knowleg of his truth, your ignorance to vndo
140 That you may be one of those numbred Christians,
Which foloweth the lambe whether he doth go,
The lambe Iesus Christ, my meaning is so,
By sure fayth & confidence in his bitter death & passyon,
The only pryce of our health and saluacion.

Iuuentus.

145 Syr, I thanke you for your herty oratyon
And now I pray you shewe me your aduisemente,
How I may liue in thys my vocacyon,
According to Goddes wil and commaundement.

Good Councell.

First of all it is moste expedient
150 That you exercise your selfe in continual prayer,
That it might please the Lord omnipotente,
To send vnto you his holy spirit and comforter:
Which wyl leade you euery day and houre,
Unto the knowledge of hys word and veritie,
155 Wherin you may learne to liue most christianly.

Iuuentus. *He kneleth.*

O Lord graunt me of thy infinite mercy,
The true knowlege of thy lawe and wyll,
And illumine my heart with thy spirit continually,
That I may be apte thy holy preceptes to fulfyl:
160 Strengthen me, that I may parseuer stil,
Thy commaundementes to obaye,
And then shal I neuer slip nor fal away.

He riseth.

Good Councell.

Ful true be these wordes, which Christ himselfe did say
He that seketh shal surely finde.

Knowledge entreth.

165 Beholde (Youth) now reioyce we may.
For I se Knowledge of God[s] Veritie stand here behinde,

He is come now to satisfye your minde,
In those thynges which you wil desire,
Therfore togither, let vs approche him nere.

Iuuentus.

170 A[h] Good Councell, now it doth appere,
That God neuer reiecteth the humbles peticion.

Knowledge.

Now the Lord blesse you al with his heauenly benediction
And with his fyery loue your heartes enflame,
That of his mercifull promises you may haue the fruition
175 The subtiltie, of the deuill, vtterly to defame:
Now good Christian audience I wyl expresse my name,
The true Knowlege of Gods Veritie, this mi name doth hyghte,
Whom God hath appoynted to geue the blind their sight.

Good Councell.

Al prayse be giuen to that Lord of myght,
180 Which hath appointed you hether at this present houre,
For I trust you will so instruct Youth a right,
That he shall lyue accordynge to Gods pleasure.

Iuuentus.

And I thanke Iesus Christ my sauiour,
That he is come to my company.

Knowledge.

185 I thanke you my frendes most hartely
For your gentil salutacion.

Iuuentus.

Sir, I wyl be so bold by your deliberation,
To open my mynd vnto you nowe,
Trustyng that by your good exhortation,
190 I shal learne those thynges which I neuer knew:
This one thynge chiefly I would learne of you,
How I may my life in this my vocation leade,
According as God hath ordeyned and decrede.

Knowledge.

The prophet Dauid saith, that the man is blessed,
195 Which doth exerceyse him selfe in the law of the Lord,
And doth not folow the way of the wicked,
As the fyrst psalme doth playnly recorde:
The foure score & .xiii. psalme therunto doth accorde,
Blessed is the man whom thou teachest, O Lord, saith he
200 To learne thy lawe, precepts, worde, or veritie,

And Christ in the Gospell sayth manyfestly.
Blessed is he which heareth the word of God & kepeth it,
That is, to beleue his word, & liue accordingly,
Declaring the fayth by the fruites of the spirite,
205 Whose fruites are these, as S. Paul to the Galathi, doth wryte:
Loue, ioye, peace, long suffering and faithfulnes
Mekenes, goodnes, temperaunce and gentilnes.

Good Councell.

By these wordes which vnto you he doth expresse,
He teacheth that you ought to haue a stedfast faith,
210 Without the which it is impossible doutelesse,
To please God, as Saint Paul sayth:

Where faith is not, godly liuyng decayeth,
For whatsoeuer is not of faith, saith S. Paul, is sinne:
But where a perfite faith is, there is good workyng.

Iuuentus.

215 It semeth to me that this is your meaning,
That when I obserue Gods commaundementes & the works
of charite,
They shal preuail vnto me nothing,
Except I beleue to be saued therby.

Knowledge.

No, no, you are deceyued very blyndly,
220 For faith in Christes merites doth onely iustify,
And make vs righteous in Goddes sight.

Iuuentus.

Why should I then in Good workes delight?
Seing I shal not be saued by them.

Good Councell.

Because they are required of all Christian men,
225 As the necessary fruites of true repentaunce.

Knowledge.

But the reward of the heauenly inheritaunce,
Is geuen vs through fayth, for Christes deseruinges,
As S. Paul declareth in the .iiii. chapter to the Romains
Therfore we ought not to worke as hierlinges:
230 Seing Christ hath purged vs once from al our wicked liuing
Let vs no more wallow therin,
But perseuer like good braunches, bearing frute in him.

Iuuentus.
Now I know where about you haue bene,
My elders neuer taught me so before.

Good Councell.
235 Though your elders wer blind, dout not you therfore
For Saint Peter sayth, vaine is the conuersations,
Which ye receiue by your elders tradicions.

Iuuentus.
I wil gladly receiue your godly admonicions,
But yet I praye you shewe me the cause,
240 That they being men of great discretions
Dyd not instructe me in Gods lawes,
Accordyng to hys wyll and ordynaunce.

Knowledge.
Bycause they them selues were wrapped in ignoraunce
Being deceyued by false preachers.

Iuuentus.
245 O Lord delyuer me from wycked teachers,
That I be not deceyued wyth theyr false doctrine.

Good Councell.
To Gods word you must only encline,
All other doctrine cleane set a parte.

Iuuentus.
Surely, that I wyll from the bottome of my heart,
250 And I thanke the liuing God which hath geuen me the
                                                        knowledge
To know his doctrine from the false & peruarte

I being yet yonge and full tender of age:
And that he hath made me partaker of the heauenly inheritage
Of his owne mercy and not of my deseruynge,
255 For hell I haue deserued by my synfull workynge.

I know ryght well my elders and parentes,
Haue of a longe tyme deceyued be,
Wyth blynd hipocrisy and supersticyous ententes,
Trustyng in theyr owne workes which is nothyng but vanitie
260 Their steppes shall not be folowed for me,
Therfore I pray you shew me a briefe conclusyon,
How I ought to lyue in Christyan relygion.

Knowledge.

The first beginning of wisdom, as saith the wise Salomon
Is to feare God wyth al thy heart and power,
265 And then ye must beleue al his promises without any exception
And that he wyll performe them both constant & sure
And then because he is thy onely sauiour,
Thou must loue him wyth al thy soule and mynde,
And thy neighbour as thy self, because he hath so assined.

Iuuentus.

270   To loue my neighbour as my self, I cannot be so kind
I pray you tel me, what meane you?

Knowledge.

My meaninge is as Christe sayth in the sixt chapiter of
                              Mathew,
To do to him as you would be done to.

Iuuentus.

I pray God geue me grace so for to do,
275 That vnto his will I may be obedient.

Good Councell [*presenting a New Testament to Iuuentus*].

    Here you shall receiue Christes testament,
    To comfort your conscience when nede shall require,
    To learne the contentes therof, se that you be diligent,
    The which al Christian men ought to desyre.
280 For it is the well, or fountayne most clere,
    Out of the which doth spryng swete consolation,
    To all those which thirst after eternal saluation.

Knowledge.

    Therin shall you fynd most holsome preseruatyon,
    Both in troubles, persecutions, sicknes & aduersitie,
285 And a sure defence in the tyme of temptacion,
    Agaynst whom the deuill cannot preuail with all his armi:
    And if you perseuer therin vnfainedly,
    It wyll set your heart at such quietnes and rest,
    Whych can neuer be turned wyth stormes nor tempest.

Good Councell.

290   Wyth this thing you must neither flatter nor iest.
    But stedfastly beleue it euery day and houre,
    And let your conuersacion openly protest,
    That of your heart it is the most precious treasure:
    And then your godly example shall other men procure,
295 To learne and exercyse the same also,
    I pray God strengthen you so for to do.

Iuuentus.

    Now for this godli knowlege which you haue brought me to
    I beseche the liuing God to reward you agayne,
    From your companye I wyl neuer depart nor go,
300 So longe as in this lyfe I do remayne:

For in thys boke I se manifest and playne,
That he that foloweth his owne lustes & imagination,
Kepeth the ready path to euerlasting dampnation,

    And he that leadeth a godly conuersation,
305 Shall be brought to suche quietnes, ioy and peace,
Which in comparison passeth all worldly gloriation,
Which can not endure but shortly cease,
Both the time and houre I may now blesse,
That I met with you father Good Councell,
310 To bring me to the knowlege of this heuenly gospell.

Knowledge.

This your profession I lyke very well,
So that you entend to liue accordyng,
I pray God your liuing do not rebell,
But euer agre vnto your saying,
315 That when ye shall make a countes or rekenyng,
Of this talent which you haue receyued,
You may be one of those with whom the Lord shal be pleased.

Good Councell.

For this conuersacion of Youth the Lords name be praised
Let vs now depart for a season. *Exit.*

Knowledge.

320   To geue God the glory it is conuenient and reason,
If you wil depart, I wyl not tary. *Exit.*

Iuuentus.

And I wil neuer forsake your company,
While I lyue in this world. *Exit.*

Here entreth the Deuill [lamenting loudly].

[Deuyl.]

    Oh oh, al to late,
325 I trow this geare wil come to naught,
    For I perceyue my power doth abate,
    For all the policie that euer I haue wrought.
    Many and sundry waies I haue sought,
    To haue the word of God deluded vtterly,
330 Oh for sorow, yet it will not be.

    I haue done the best that I can,
    And my ministers also in euery place,
    To roote it clene from the heart of man,
    And yet for all that it florisheth apace:
335 I am sore in drede to shew my face,
    My auctoritie and workes are so greatly dispised,
    My inuentions, and al that euer I haue deuised.

    Oh oh, ful well I know the cause,
    That my estimacion doth thus decay.
340 The olde people would beleue stil in my lawes,
    But the yonger sort leade them a contrary way
    They wyll not beleue they playnly say,
    In old traditions and made by men,
    But they wyll lyue as the scripture teacheth them.

345   Out I crie vpon them, they do me open wrong,
    To bring vp theyr children thus in knowlage,
    For if they wil not folow my waies when they are yong
    It is hard turning them when they come to age:
    I must nedes fynd some meanes this matter to swage,
350 I meane to turne theyr hartes from the scripture quyte
    That in carnall plesures they may haue more delight.

Well I will go taste to enfect this Youth,
Through the entisement of my sonne Hipocrisie,
And worke sume proper feate to stop his mouth.
355 That he may lede his life carnally:
I had neuer more nede my matters to apply,
Oh my chyld Hipocrisie, where art thou?
I charge the of my blessing appere before me now.

Here entreth Hypocrisie [as the Deuyl conjures].

Hypocrisie.
Oh oh quod ha, kepe agayne the sowe.
360 I come as fast as I can I warrant you,
Where is he that hath the sowe to sell?
I wil geue him money if I lyke her well,
Whether it be sowe or hogge, I do not greatly care,
For by my occupacion I am a bochare.

Deuyl.
365 Oh my child, how doest thou fare?

Hypocrisie.
Sancti amen, who haue we there?
By the masse I wil bie none of thy ware,
Thou art a chapman for the deuell.

Deuyl.
What my sonne, canst thou not tel,
370 Who is here, and what I am?
I am thine owne father Sathan.

Hypocrisie.
Be you so syr? I crye you mercy than,
You may say I am homely, & lacke learnyng,

To liken my fathers voice vnto a sowes groninge,
375 But I pray you shew me the cause, and why
That you called me hether so hastely.

Deuyl.

A Hipocrisie, I am vndone vtterly.

Hypocrisie.

Utterly vndone, nay stop there hardely,
For I my selfe do know the contrary,
380 By dayly experience:
Do not I yet raigne abrode?
And as longe as I am in the worlde,
You haue som treasure & substaunce.

I suppose I haue bene the flower,
385 In settyng furth thy lawes & power,
Wythout any delay
By the masse if I had not bene,
Thou haddest not benne worthe a flaunders pin,
At thys present day.

390   The time were to long nowe to declare,
How many and great the number are,
Which haue desceiued be:
And brought cleane from Gods lawe,
Unto thy yoke and awe,
395 Through the intisement of me.

I haue bene busyed, since the world began,
To graffe thy lawes in the heart of man,
Where they ought to be refused:
And I haue so mingled Gods commaundementes,
400 Wyth vaine zeales, and blynd intentes,
That they be greatly abused.

    I set vp great ydolatry,
With al kind of filthy Sodometry,
To geue mankynde a fall:
405 And I brought vp such supersticion
Under the name of holynes and religion,
That deceyued almost all.

    As holy Cardinals, holy Popes,
Holy vestimentes, holy copes,
410 Holy Harmettes and Friers,
Holy priestes, holy bisshopes,
Holy Monkes, holy abbottes,
Yea, and al obstinate lyers.

    Holy pardons, holy beades.
415 Holy Saintes, holy Images,
With holy, holy bloud
Holy stockes, holy stones:
Holy cloughtes, holy bones:
Yea, and holy holy wood.

420   Holy skinnes, holy bulles,
Holy Rochettes, and coules:
Holy crouches and staues:
Holy hoodes, holy cappes:
Holy Miters, holy hattes:
425 And good holy holy knaues.

    Holy dayes, holy fastinges:
Holy twitching, holy tastynges:
Holy visions and sightes:
Holy waxe, holy leade:
430 Holy water, holy breade:
To driue away spirites.

    Holy fyre, holy palme:
    Holy oyle, holy creame
    And holy asshes also:
435 Holy brouches, holy ringes:
    Holy knelinge, holy sensynges:
    And a hundred trim trams mo.

    Holy crosses, holy belles:
    Holy reliques, holy iewels:
440 Of mine own inuencion:
    Holy candels, holy tapers:
    Holy parchementes, holy papers:
    Had not you a holy sonne?

Deuyl.
    All these thynges which thou hast done
445 My honour and lawes hath maintayned,
    But now, Oh alas, one thinge is begune,
    By the which my kingdome is greatly decayed
    I shal lese al I am sore afrayde.
    Excepte thy helpc I know right playne,
450 I shal neuer be able to recouer it againe.

    Gods word is so greatly spronge vp in Youth,
    That he litle regardeth my lawes or me,
    He telleth his parentes that it is very truth,
    That they of long time haue deceyued be:
455 He sayth according to Chrystes veritye,
    All his doinges he wil ordre and frame,
    Mortifying the flesshe with the lustes of the same.

Hypocrisie.
    A syra, there beginneth the game,

What, is Iuuentus become so tame?
460 To be a newe gospeller?

Deuyl.
As fast as I do make, he doth marre,
He hath folowed so longe the steppes of Good Councel,
That Knowledge and he together doth dwel,
For who is so busye in euery place, as Youth,
465 To reade and declare the manyfest truth?
But oh Hipocrisye if thou could stoppe his mouth,
Thou shuldest wyn my hart for euer.

Hypocrisie.
What would you haue me to do in the matter?
Shew me therin your aduisement.

Deuyl.
470 I would haue the go incontinent.
And worke some craft, feate or polycye,
To set Knowledge and him at contrauersye,
And his company thy selfe greatly vse,
That Gods word he may clene abuse.

Hypocrisie.
475 At your request I wyl not refuse,
To do that thynge which in me doth lye,
Dout ye not but I wyll excuse,
Those thynges whych he doth playnly deny.
And I wyll handle my matters so craftely,
480 That ere he commeth to mannes state:
Gods word and his liuing shalbe cleane at the bate.

Deuyl.
Thou shalt haue my blessyng both early and late,
And be cause thou shalt al my counsel kepe,
Thou shalt call thy name Frendshyp.

Hypocrisie.
485 By the masse it is a name full mete,
For my proper and amyable person.

Deuyl.
Oh, farewell farewell my sonne,
Spede thy busines, for I must be gone. *Exit.*

Hypocrisie.
I warrant you, let me alone,
490 I will be wyth Iuuentus anone,
And that ere he be ware:
And I wysse if he walke not streight,
I wyll vse such a sleight,
That shall trap him in a snare.

495 How shall I bring this geare to passe?
I can tell now by the masse,
Without any more aduysement:
I wyl infect hym wyth wicked company,
Whose conuersation shalbe so fleshly,
500 Yea, able to ouercome an innocent.

Thys wicked Felowship,
Shall hym company kepe,
For a while:
And then I wyll brynge in,
505 Abhominable Lyuyng,
Hym to beguile.

Wyth wordes fayre I wyll hym tyse,
Tellyng hym of a gyrle nyse,
Which shall hym somwhat moue:
510 Abhominable Liuinge though she be,
Yet he shall no other wayes se,
But she is for to loue.

She shall him procure,
To lyue in pleasure,
515 After his owne phantesy:
And my matter to frame,
I wyll call her name,
Unknowen Honestie.

Thus will I conuey,
520 My matter I say
Somewhat hansomely,
That through wicked Felowship:
And false pretende Frendship,
Youth shal lyue carnally.

525   Trudge Hipocrisie trudge,
Thou art a good drudge,
To serue the Deuill:
If thou shouldest lye and lurke,
And not entende thy worke,
530 Thy maister should do ful euill.

Here entreth Youth to whom Hypocrisie yet speaketh.

What mayster Youth.
Wel I met by my truth,
And whether away?
You are the last man,

535 Which I talked on,
    I sware by thys day.

    Me thought by your face,
    Ere you came in place,
    It should be you:
540 Therfore I dyd abyde,
    Here in this tyde,
    For your comming, this is true.

Iuuentus.
    For your gentlenes, syr, most hertely I thanke you,
    But yet you must hold me somwhat excused,
545 For to my symple knowledge I neuer knewe,
    That you and I together were acquainted,
    But neuertheles, if you do it renew,
    Old acquaintaunce wil sone be remembred.

Hypocrisie.
    Ah nowe I se well Youth is fethered,
550 And his crums he hath well gathered,
    Since I spake with him last:
    A pore mans tale can not now be herd,
    As in tymes past.

    I crye you mercy, I was sumwhat bolde
555 Thinking that your mastership would
    Not haue bene so straunge:
    But now I perceyue that promocion,
    Causeth both man, maners, and fashion,
    Greatly for to chaunge.

Iuuentus.

560 You are to blame thus me to calenge,
For I thinke I am not he which you take me for.

Hypocrisie.

Yes I haue knowen you euer since you were bore,
Your age is yet vnder a score.
Which I can well remember:
565 I wisse, I wisse you and I,
Many a time haue bene ful mery,
When you wer yong and tender.

Iuuentus.

Then I pray you let vs reason no lenger,
But fyrst shew your nominacion.

Hypocrisie.

570 Of my name to make declaracion
Wythout any dissimulacion,
I am called Frendshyp:
Although I be simple and rude of fashion
Yet by linage and generacion,
575 I am nie kin to your mastershyp.

Iuuentus.

What Frendshyp.
I am glad to se that you be mery,
By my truth I had almost you forgot,
By long absence brought out of memory.

Hypocrisie.

580 By the masse I loue you so hartely,
That there is none so welcome to my cumpany,
I pray you tel me, whether are you going?

Iuuentus.

My entention is to go hear a preachinge.

Hypocrisie.

A preaching quod ha, ah good little one.
585 By Christ she wil make you cry out of the wynnyng,
If you folow her instructions so early in the morning.

Iuuentus.

Full great I do abhorre this your wycked sayinge,
For no dout they encrease much sinne and vice,
Therfore I pray you, shew not your meanyng,
590 For I delight not in such folyshe fantesies.

Hypocrisie.

Surely, then you are the more vnwyse,
You may haue a spyrt amongest them now and then,
Why should not you as well as other men?

Iuuentus.

As for those fylthy doinges, I vtterly detest them,
595 I will heare no more of your wicked communycacyon.

Hypocrisie.

If I may be so bold by your deliberation
What wyl you do at a preaching?

Iuuentus.

Learne some holsome and godly teachyng,
Of the true minister of Christes gospell.

Hypocrisie.

600 Tush, what he will say I know ryght well,
He wyll say that God is a good man,
He can make him no better, and say the best he can.

Iuuentus.

I know that, but what then?
The more that Gods word is preached and taught,
605 The greater the occasion is to al Christen men,
To forsake their sinful liuinges both wicked, vile & naught:
And to repent their former euils which they haue wrought
Trusting by Christes death to be redemed,
And he that thys doth, shal neuer be disceiued.

Hypocrisie.

610 Well sayd maister doctor, well sayd,
By the masse we must haue you, into the pulpyt,
I pray you be remembred, and couer your head,
For in dede you haue nede to kepe in your wyt,
A Sirra, who would haue thought it,
615 That Youth had bene such a well learned man?
Let me se your portous gentle Sir Iohn.

Iuuentus.

No, it is not a boke for you to loke on,
You ought not to iest wyth Gods testament.

Hypocrisie.

What man I pray you be content,

620 For I do nothyng els but say my phantasie.
But yet if you would do after my aduisement,
In that matter you should not be so busy,
Was not your father as well learned as ye?
And if he had said then, as you haue now done,
625 I wisse he had bene like to make a burne.

Iuuentus.

It were muche better for me, then to returne,
From my faith in Christe, & the profession of his worde.

Hypocrisie.

Whether is better a halter or a corde,
I can not tel. I sweare by Goddes mother,
630 But I thynke you,wil haue the one or the other.
Wil you lose al your frendes good wyll,
To continue in that opinion still?
Was there not as wel learned men before as now?
Yea, and better to, I may say to you,
635 And they taught the yonger sort, of people,
By the elders to take an example.
And if I did not loue you as nature doth me bynde,
You should not know so muche of my mynde.

Iuuentus.

Whether were I better to be ignoraunt and blynd,
640 And to be dampned in hell for infidelitie,
Or to learne godly knowledge, wherin I shall fynde,
The right pathway to eternal felicitie?

Hypocrisie.

Can you denie but it is your duetie.
Unto your elders to be obedient?

Iuuentus.
645 I graunt I am bound to obey my parentes,
In all thinges honest and lawfull.

Hypocrisie.
Lawfull quod ha, a foole foole,
Wylt thou set men to scoole,
When they be olde?
650 I may say to you secretly,
The world was neuer mery,
Since children were so bolde:

Now euery boy wyl be a teacher
The father a foole, and the chyld a preacher,
655 This is preaty geare
The foule presumption of youth
Wyl turne shortly to great ruth
I fere, I feare, I feare.

Iuuentus.
The sermone wil be done ere I can come there,
660 I care not greatly whether I go or no,
And yet for my promise, by God I sweare,
There is no remedy but I must nedes go:
Of my companions ther wyl be mo,
And I promysed them by Goddes grace.
665 To mete them there as the sermon was.

Hypocrisie.
For once breakyng promise do not you passe,
Make some excuse the matter to cease,
What haue they to do?
And you and I were I wote where,

670 We would be as mery as there,
    Yea, and meryer to.

Iuuentus.
    I would gladly in your company go.
    But if my companions shoulde chaunce to se,
    They would report full euyl by me:
675 And peraduenture if I should it vse,
    My company they would cleane refuse.

Hypocrisie.
    What, are those felowes so curyous,
    That your selfe you cannot excuse?
    I wyll teache you the matter to conuey,
680 Do what your own lust, & say as they say
    And if you be reproued with your owne affinitie,
    Byd them plucke the beame out of theyr owne eye,

    The old popish priestes mocke and despyse,
    And the ignoraunt people that beleue their lyes,
685 Call them papistes, hipocrites, & cloyncs of the plough,
    Face out the matter, and then good ynough,
    Let your booke at your gyrdle be tyed,
    Or els in your bosome that he may be spyed,

    And then it wyl be sayd both with youth and age,
690 Yonder felow hath an excellent knowledge,
    Tusshe tusshe.
    I could so beate the busshe,
    That al shuld be flusshe,
    That euer I dyd.

Iuuentus.
695 Now by my truth you are meryly disposed,
Let vs go thether as you thynke best.

Hypocrisie.
How saye you, shal we go to breakefast?
Will you go to the pye feast,
Or by the masse if thou wilt be my gest,
700 It shal cost the nothyng,
I haue a furny carde in a place,
That wil bare a turne besides the ace

She puruyes now a pace,
For my commynge:
705 And if thou wilt iybbere as well as I,
We shal haue mery company,
And I warrant the yf we haue not a pye,
We shal haue a puddinge.

Iuuentus.
By the masse that meate I loue aboue al thynge,
710 You may drawe me aboute the toune with a puddynge:

Hypocrisie.
Then you shal se my cunnyng.
A poore shyft for a liuinge,
Amongest poore men vsed is,

> *Here entreth Felowshyp. [He does not see Hypocrisie and Iuuentus.]*

The kynde heart of hyrs,
715 Hath eased my purse,
Many a time ere this.

Felowshyp.

I meruayle gretly where Frendshyp is,
He promised to mete me here eare this time
I beshrew his heart that his promis doth mys,
720 And then be ye sure it shall not be mine.

Hypocrisie. *[He comes forward.]*

Yes Felowshyp that it shalbe thine
For I haue taried here this hour or twayne,
And this honest gentilman in my company hath bene,
To abide your comming this thing is playne.

Felowshyp.

725   By the masse if you chyde I wylt be gone agayne,
For in fayth Frendshyp I may say to the
I loue not to be there where chiders be.

Hypocrisie.

No God it knoweth you are as ful of honesty,
As a mary bone is ful of honey,
730 But syra I pray you bid this gentilman welcome,
For he is desirous in your company to come
I tell you he is a man of the ryght makyng,
And one that hath excellent lernynge,
At his gyrdle he hath such a boke
735 That the popysshe priestes dare not on hym loke.
This is a felow for the nones.

Felowshyp.

I loue him the better by dogs precious bones,
You are hertely welcom as I may saye, *[He greets Iuuentus.]*

I shal desyre you of better acquantaunce,
740 That of your company be bolde I maye,
You may be sure if in me it lye,
To do you pleasure you should it fynde,
For by the masse I loue you, both with hert and mynde.

Iuuentus.

To say the same to you, your gentlenes doth me bynde
745 And I thanke you hertely for your kindnes.

Hypocrisie.

Wyl you se thys gentelmans fynes,
Your gentilnes and your kyndnes,
I thanke him and I thanke you,
And I thynke if the truth were sought,
750 The one bad, and the other naught,
Neuer a good I make God a vow,
But yet Felowshyp tel me one thing,
Dyd you se litle Besse this morning?
We should haue our brekfast yester night she sayde,
755 But she hath forgotten it now, I am afrayd.

Felowshyp.

Her promise shalbe perfourmed and payd,
For I spake with her synce the time I rose
And then she told me how the matter goes:
We must be with her betwene eyght and nine,
760 And then her Maister & Mystres wyl be at the preching.

Iuuentus.

I purposed my selfe there to haue bene,
But this man prouoked me to the contrary
And told me that we shuld haue mery company.

Felowshyp.
Mery quod ha, we can not chuse but be mery,
765 For there is such a gyrle, where as we go,
Which wil make vs to be mery whether we will or no.

Hypocrisie.
The ground is the better on the which she doth go.
For she will make better chere with that litle which she can get
Then many a one can with a great banket of meat.

Iuuentus.
770   To be in her company my hart is set,
Therfore I pray you let vs be gone.

Felowshyp.
She will come for vs her selfe anone
For I told her before where we would stande
And then she sayd she would becke vs with her hande.

Iuuentus.
775   Now by the masse I perceyue that she is a gallaunde,
What wyl she take paynes to come for vs hether?

Hypocrisie.
Yea I warrant you, therfore you muste be famylier with her
When she commeth in place,
You must her embrace,
780 Sumwhat hansomlye,
Leste she thinke it daunger,
Bicause you are a straunger
To come in your companye.

Iuuentus.
Yea by Gods foote that I wyl be busye
785 And I may saye to you I can play the knaue secretly.

[Enter Abhominable Liuing.]

Abhominable Liuing.
Hem, come away quickly
The backe dore is open I dare not tarry,
Come Felowship come on a waye.

Hypocrisie.
What Unknowen Honestie a worde [I pray]
790 You shal not go yet by God I sweare,
Here is none but your frindes, you nede not to fraie,
Although this straunge yonge gentylman be here.

Iuuentus.
I trust in me she wyl thynke no daunger,
For I loue wel the company of fayre women.

Abhominable Liuing.
795 Who you, nay ye are suche a holy man,
That to touche one ye dare not be bolde,
I thynke you would not kisse a yonge woman,
Yf one would giue you .xx. pound in goulde.

Iuuentus.
Yes by the masse that I would,
800 I could fynde in my hert to kisse you in your smocke.

Abhominable Liuing.
My backe is brode inough to bare awaye that mocke
For one hath tolde me many a time,
That you haue said you wold vse no such wantons company as
myne.

Iuuentus.
By dogs precious woundes that was som whorson villain
805 I wyll neuer eate meate that shal do me good,
Tyl I haue cut his fleshe by gogs precyous blud,
Tell me I praye you who it was,
And I wyl trim the knaue by the blessed masse.

Abhominable Liuing.
Tush as for that do not you passe,
810 That which I tolde you was but for loue.

Hypocrisie.
She did nothing else but proue,
Whether a litle thinge would you moue,
To be angry and frettc,
What and if one had sayed so
815 Let such triflyng matters go,
And be good to mens flesh for al that.

Iuuentus kisseth Abhominable Liuing.

Iuuentus.
To kysse her since she came I had cleane forgot
You are wel come to my company.

Abhominable Liuing.
Syr I thanke you most hartely,

820 By your kindnes it doth apere.

Hypocrisie.
What a hurly burly is here,
Smicke smacke and all this gere,
You will to ticke tacke I fere,
If you had time,
825 Well wanton well,
I wysse I can tel,
That such smocke smell
Will set your nose out of tune.

Abhominable Liuing.
What man you nede not to fume.
830 Seing he is come into my company now,
He is as well welcome as the best of you,
And if it lye in me to do him pleasure,
He shal haue it you may be sure.

Felowshyp.
Then old acquaintaunce is cleane out of fauour.
835 Lo Frendshyp, this geare goeth with a sleight
He hath driuen vs twayne out of conceite.

Hypocrisie.
Out of conceite, quod ha no no,
I dare wel saye she thynketh not so,
How say you Unknowen Honestie?
840 Do not you loue Felowship and me?

Abhominable Liuing.
Ye by the masse I loue you al thre,
But yet in dede yf I should say the truth,
Amongest al other welcome Mayster Youth.

[Iuuentus] he kisseth [Abhominable Liuing].

Iuuentus.
Ful greatly I do delight to kisse your plesaunt mouth
845 I am not able your kyndnes to recompence,
I long to talke with you secretly, therfore let vs go hence.

Abhominable Liuing.
I agre to that, for I would not for .xx. pence,
That it were knowne where I haue bene.

Hypocrisie.
What and it were knowne it is no deadly synne,
850 As for my parte I do not greatly care,
So that they fynd not your proper buttockes bare.

Abhominable Liuing.
Now much fye vpon you how baudy you are,
I wysse Frendship it mought haue bene spoken at twise,
What thinke you for your sayieng that the people wil surmise.

Iuuentus.
855 Who dare be so bold vs to despise?
And if I may heare a knaue speake one worde,
I wyll runne thorow his chekes with my sword.

Felowshyp.
This is an ernest fellow of Gods worde,
Se I pray you, how he is disposed to fyghte.

Iuuentus.
860 Why, shuld I not and if my cause be ryght,
What and if a knaue do me begyle?

Shal I stand crouching like an owle,
No no, then you might count me a very cowe,
I knowe what belongeth to Gods lawe as well as you.

Abhominable Liuing.

865   Your wit therin greatly I do alowe,
For and yf I were a man as you are,
I would not sticke to geue a blowe,
To teache other knaues to beware.
I beshrew you twise and if you do spare
870 But lay lode on the flesshe what so euer befal,
You haue strength inough to do it with all.

Felowshyp.

Let vs depart, and if that we shall,
Come on maisters we twayne will go before.

Iuuentus.

Nay nay my frynde stoppe there,
875 It is not you that shall haue her awaye,
She shal go with me and if she go to daye.

Hypocrisie.

She will go with none of you I dare well saye,
She will go with me before you both.

Abhominable Liuing.

To forsake any of your company I wold be very loth
880 Therfore I will folow you all thre.

Hypocrisie.

Now I beshrew his herte, that to that wil not agree,
But yet because the time shal not seme very longe,
Or eare we departe let vs haue a mery songe.

They synge as foloweth.

    Why should not youth fulfyl his owne mynde,
885 As the course of nature doth him bynde,
    Is not euery thyng ordayned to do his kinde?
    Report me to you, reporte me to you.

    Do not the flouers sprynge freshe and gaye,
    Pleasaunt and swete in the month of Maye?
890 And when their time cometh they fayd awaye,
    Report me to you, reporte me to you.

    Be not the trees in wynter bare?
    Like vnto their kynde, such they are,
    And when they springe, their fruites declare.
895 Report me to you, reporte me to you.

    What should youth do, with the fruites of age,
    But liue in pleasure in hys passage,
    For when age commeth his lustes wyll swage,
    Report me to you, rcport me to you.

They go furth [singing].

900   Why shuld not youth fulfyl his owne mynde
    As the course of nature doth hym bynde,
    [Is not euery thyng ordayned to do his kinde?
    Report me to you, reporte me to you.]   *[Exeunt.]*

Here entreth Good Councell [lamenting].

[Good Councell.]

O mercyful Lord who can ceace to lamente,
905 Or kepe his hart from continual mournynge,
To se how Youth is fallen from thy word & testament.
And wholly enclined to Abhominable Liuinge,
He liueth nothyng accordyng to hys professyng.
But alas his lyfe is, to thy word abusion,
910 Except thy great mercy, to his vtter confusion.

O where is now the godly conuersation
Which shuld be amonge the professors of thy worde,
O where may a man find now one faythful congregation
That is not enfected with dissention or discorde?
915 Or amongest whome are al vices vtterly abhored?
O where is the brotherly loue betwene man and man?
We may lamente the tyme our vyce began.

O where is the peace & mekenes, longe sufferinge &
temperaunce
Which are the fruites of Gods holy spirit?
920 With whome is the flesshe brought vnder obedience,
Or who readeth the scripture to the intent to folow it?
Who vseth not now couetousnes and disceite,
Who geueth vnto the poore that which is dewe?
I thinke in this world, there be now but a fewe.

925   O where is the godli example that parentes shuld giue,
Unto their yonge familie, by godly & vertuous liuing?
Alas how wickedly do they them selues liue,
Without any fear of God, or his righteous threatening
They haue no respect vnto the dreadfull rekenyng,
930 Which shal be required of vs, when the Lord shal come,
As a rightful iudge at the day of Dome.

O what a ioyful syght was it for to se,
When Youth began Gods worde to embrace?
Then he promised godly Knowledge and me,
935 That from our instructions he wold neuer turn his face
But now he walketh, alas: in the vngodlies chase,
Heaping sinne vpon sinne vice vpon vyce,
He that liueth most vngodly is counted most wyse.

Here entreth Iuuentus.

Iuuentus.
Who is here playing at the Dice?
940 I heard one speake of synnes and sice,
His wordes did me entice,
Hither to come.

Good Councell.
A Youth, Youth, whether doest thou runne?
Greatly I do bewayle thy miserable estate,
945 The terrible plagues, which in Gods law are written,
Hang ouer thy head both early and late:
O fleshly Capernite, stubburne and obstinate,
Thou haddest leuer forsake Christ thy sauiour & kyng,
Then thy fleshly swinish lustes, & Abhominable Liuinge.

Iuuentus.
950 What old hoorson, art thou a chiding?
I wil play a spyrt, why should I not?
I set not a mite by thy checkyng,
What hast thou to do and if I lose my cote:
I wyll trill the bones while I haue one grote,
955 And when there is no more inke in the pen,
I wyll make a shift as wel as other men.

Good Councell.
Then I perceiue you haue forgotten cleane,
The promise that you made vnto Knowledge & me,
You sayd such fleshly fruites shuld not be sene,
960 But to Gods word your lyfe should agre:
Ful true be the wordes of the prophet Osey,
No verytie nor knowledge of God is now in the land,
But abhominable vices hath gotten the vpper hand.

Iuuentus.
Your mynd therin I do wel vnderstand,
965 You go about my liuing to despyse,
But you wil not se the beames in your own eies.

Good Councell.
The Deuil hath you disceiued which is the auctour of lies
And trapt you in hys snare of wicked Hypocrisye,
Therfore al that euer you do deuise
970 Is to maintayne your fleshly libertie.

Iuuentus.
I meruaile why you do thus reproue me,
Wherin do I my life abuse?

Good Councell.
Your whole conuersacion I may well accuse,
As in my conscience iust occasion I fynd,
975 Therfore be not offended, although I expresse my mind.

Iuuentus.
By the masse if thou tel not truth, I wil not be behind,
To touch you as wel agayne.

Good Councell.

For this thing most chiefly I do complayne,
Haue you not professed the knowlege of Christes gospel
980 And yet I thinke no more vngodlines doth raigne,
In any wycked heathen, Turke or infidell:
Who can deuise that sinne or euil,
That you practise not from day to day?
Yea, and count it nothyng but a iest or a play.

985 Alas, what wantonnes remaineth in your fleshe?
How desirous are you, to accomplish your owne will?
What pleasure & delight haue you in wickednes?
How diligent are you, your lustes to fulfil?
S. Paul saith that you ought your fleshly lustes to kil
990 But vnto his teaching your life ye wyl not frame,
Therfore in vayne you beare a Christians name.

Rede the .v. to the Galathians, & there you shall se,
That the flesh rebelleth agaynst the spyrit,
And that your own flesh is your most vtter enemy,
995 If in your soules helth you do delight:
The time were to long now to recite,
What whordom, vncleanes & filthy communicacion,
Is despersed with Youth, in euery congregacion.

To speke of pride, enuye, and abhominable othes,
1000 They are the common practises of Youth,
To aduaunce your flesh, you cut & iagge your clothes,
And yet ye are a great gospeller in the mouth:
What shal I say for this blaspheming the truth,
I wyl shew you what S. Paul doth declare
1005 In his epistle to the Hebrues, & the .x. chapiter.

For him sayth he, which doth willingly sin or consent
After he hath receyued the knowledge of the veritie,
Remaineth no more sacrifice, but a fearful looking for
                                      iudgement,
And a terrible fier, which shal consume the aduersary:
1010 And Christ saith that this blasphemy,
Shal neuer be pardoned nor forgiuen,
In this world, nor in the world to come.

Iuuentus.
Alas alas what haue I wrought and done?
Here in this place I wil fal doune desperate,
1015 To aske for mercy now I know it is to late.

He lyeth downe.

Alas alas that euer I was begat,
I wold to God I had neuer bene borne,
Al faithful men that behold this wretched state,
May very iustly laugh me to scorne:
1020 They may say my time I haue euyl spent and worne,
Thus in my first age, to worke my owne destruction,
In the eternal paynes is my part and portion.

Good Councell.
Why Youth art thou fallen into desperation?
What man plucke vp thin heart, and rise,
1025 Although thou se nothyng now, but thy condempnation,
Yet it may please God agayn to open thy eies:
Ah wretched creature, what doest thou surmise?
Thinkest ye not that Gods mercy doth excede thy synne?
Remembre his merciful promises & comfort thi self in him.

Iuuentus.

1030   O sir, this state is so miserable the which I lye in,
That my comfort and hope from me is seperated,
I would to God I had neuer bene,
Wo worth the time that euer I was created.

Good Councell.

A[h] fayre vessell vnfaithful and feinte hearted,
1035 Doest thou thinke that God is so mercyles,
That when the sinner doth repente, and is conuerted,
That he will not fulfyl his mercyful promises?

Iuuentus.

Alas syr, I am in suche heauines,
That his promises I cannot remembre.

Good Councell.

1040   In thy wickednes continue no lenger,
But trust in the Lord without any feare,
And his merciful promises shall shortly appeare.

Iuuentus.

I would beleue if I might them heare,
Wyth al my heart, power and mynde.

Good Councell.

1045   The liuing God hath him hether assyned:
Lo, where he commeth euen here by,

Here entreth Gods Mercyfull Promyses.

Therfore marke his sainges diligently.

[Gods Mercyfull Promyses.]
The Lorde by hys prophet Ezechiel, sayeth in this wise
playnly
As in the .xxxiii. chapter it doth appere,
1050 Be conuerted O ye children, & turne vnto me,
And I shal remeady the cause of your departure.
And also he sayeth in the .xviii. chapter,
I do not delight in a sinners death.
But that he should conuert & liue, thus the Lord sayth.

Iuuentus.
1055   Then must I geue neither creadite nor fayth,
Unto Saint Paules sayinge which thys man did alege.

Gods Mercyfull Promy[ses].
Yes, you must credite them, accordyng vnto knowledge
For Saint Paul speketh of those which resiste the truth by
vyolence
And so end theyr liues without repentaunce.
1060 Thus Saint Augustine doth them define.

If vnto the Lordes word you do your eares encline,
And obserue those thinges which he hath commaunded
This sinfull state in the which you haue lien,
Shal be forgotten and neuer more remembred,
1065 And Christ him selfe in the gospell hath promised,
That he which in him vnfaynedly doth beleue,
Although he were dead, yet shal he liue.

Iuuentus. *He riseth.*
These comfortable sayings doth me greatly moue,
To arise from this wretched place.

Gods Mercyfull Promyses.

1070 For me his mercy sake thou shalte obtayne his grace,
And not for thine owne desertes, this must thou knowe,
For my sake alone he shal receyue solace,
For my sake alone he wil the mercy shew,
Therfore to him as it is most due,
1075 Geue most harty thankes, with hart vnfayned,
Whose name for euer more be praysed.

Good Councell.

The prodigal sonne as in Luke we rede
Which in vicious liuing his goodes doth wast,
As sone as his liuing he had remembred,
1080 To confesse his wretchednes he was not agast
Wherfore his father louingly him embrast,
And was right ioyfull the text sayth playne
Bycause his sonne was returned agayne.

Iuuentus.

O synfull flesh, thy pleasures are but vayne,
1085 Now I find it true, as the scripture doth saye,
Brode & pleasaunt is the path which ledeth vnto payne
But vnto eternall life ful narowe is the waye.
He that is not led by Gods spyrite surely goeth astraye,
And al that euer he doth shalbe clene abhorde,
1090 Although he bragge & bost neuer so much of Gods word.

O subtil Sathan, ful deceitful is thy snare,
Who is able thy falshed to disclose?
What is the man that thou doest fauour or spare,
And doest not tempt him eternal ioyes to lose?
1095 Not one in the world, surely I suppose,

Therfore happy is the man whych doth truely wayte,
Alwayes to refuse thy deceytful and crafty bayte.

When I had thought to lyue most Christyanly,
And folowed the steppes of Knowledge and Good Councell,
1100 Ere I was ware thou haddest deceyued me,
And brought me into the path which leadeth vnto hell:
And of an earnest professor of Christes gospell,
Thou madest me an ypocrite, blynd and peruert,
And from vertue vnto vice, ye hadst cleane turned mi hert.

1105 First, by Hipocrisie thou diddest me moue,
The mortification of the flesh cleane to forsake,
And wanton desyres to embrace and loue,
Alas to thynke on it my heart doth yet quake,
Under the title of Frendshyp to me he spake,
1110 And so to wicked Felowship dyd me brynge,
Which brought me cleane to Abhominable Liuyng.

Thus I say, Sathan did me disceiue,
And wrapped me in sinne many a fold,
The steppes of Good Councel I dyd forsake and leaue.
1115 And forgot the words which before to me he told:
The fruites of a true Christian, in me waxed cold,
I folowed myne owne lustes, the fleshe I dyd not tame,
And had them in dirision which would not do the same.

Yet it hath pleased God of his endles mercy
1120 To geue me respite my lyfe to amende,
From the bottome of my herte I repent my iniquitie,
I wyll walke in hys lawes vnto my liues ende:
From his holy ordinaunce I wil neuer dicend,

But my whole delight shal be to liue therin,
1125 Utterly abhoring al filthines and synne.

[Iuuentus addresses the audience directly.]

All Christen people which be here present,
May learne by me, Hipocrise to know,
With the which the Deuil, as with a poyson most pestilent
Dayly seketh al men to ouerthrow:
1130 Credite not al thynges vnto the outward shew,
But trie them with Gods word, that squire & rule moste iust
Which neuer disceiueth them that in him put their trust.

Let not flatteryng Frendshyp, nor yet wicked company
Perswade you in no wyse, Gods word to abuse
1135 But se that ye stand stedfastly vnto the viritie,
And according to the rule therof, your doings frame & vse
Neither Kinred nor Felowship shal you excuse,
When you shal appere before the iudgement seat,
But your own secret conscience shal then geue an audite.

1140   All you that be yong, whom I do now represent,
Set your delite both day & nyght, on Christes testament
If pleasure you tickle, be not fickle, & sodenly slyde,
But in Gods feare euery where, se that you abide,
In your tender age, seke for knowledge, & after wisdom rune,
1145 And in your olde age, teache your familye, to do as you
                                haue don
Your bodyes subdue, vnto vertue, delite not in vaynity

Say not I am yong, I shal liue long, lest your dais shortened
                                be
Do not encline, to spend the time, in wanton toies & nyce,

For idlenes doth encrease much wickednes and vyce,
1150 Do not delay the tyme, and say, my ende is not nere,
For with short warning, the Lords comming shal sodenli apere
God giue vs grace, his word to embrace & to liue therafter
That bi the same, his holy name, may be praised euer.

Good Councell.

Now let vs make our supplications together,
1155 For the prosperous estate of our noble & vertuous king
That in his godly procedynges he may stil perseuer,
Which seketh the glory of God aboue al other thing,
O Lord endue his hert, with true vnderstanding,
And geue him a prosperous life, long ouer vs to raigne
1160 To gouerne & rule his people as a worthy captayne.

Iuuentus.

Also, let vs pray for al the nobilitie of this realme,
And namely for those, whom his grace hath auctorised,
To mayntayne the publike wealth ouer vs & them,
That they may se his gracious actes published,
1165 And that they, being truly admonisshed,
By the complaint of them which are wrongfulli opprest
May seke a reformation, and se it redrest.

Good Councell.

Then shall this land enioy great quietnes & rest,
And geue vnto God most herty thankes therfore,
1170 To whom be honour, prayse and glory for euermore.
Finis. quod R. Weuer.

Imprinted at London
in Paules churche yeard, by Abraham
Uele, at the sygne of the Lambe

Textual Notes

0. The Prologue of the messenger.] *centered and preceded by paragraph sign in C, A;* The Prologue of ye messenger. *in margin opposite ll. 1-2 in V. Biblical references omitted in A; in smaller type opposite ll. 2-3 in V, C.* Gene. viii.] *V;* gene. viii *C.* Iere. xvii.] *V;* Iere. xiiii *C (wrong reference).* Eccle. xxx.] Eccle, xxx. *V;* Eccle. xxx *C.*
1. prone] prone, *V, C, A.*
2. from] *C, A;* frō *V.*
3. withdrawen] *A;* wtdrawen, *V;* withdrawen, *C.*
5. In] An *V, A;* And *C.*
10. refuse] refuse, *V, C, A.*
11. Gods] *C, A;* gods *V.*
12. drawe] drawe, *V;* draw *C;* draw, *A.*
13. By grace . . . by nature] (By grace) . . . (by nature) *V;* (By grace(. . . (by nature *C;* By Grace . . . by Nature *A.*   goodnes:] *C;* goodnes? *V;* goodnes, *A.*
15. best] *C, A;* best, *V.*
18. the] ye *V, C, A.*
19. Youth] youth *V, C, A.*
20. Good Counsell] good counsell *V, C;* good counsel *A.*   conuersation] cōuersation *V, C, A.*
21. inclination.] inclination, *V;* inclination *C, A.*
22. Sathan] *C, A;* Sothan *V.*   Hipocrisy,] hipocrisy *V;* Hipocrisy *C, A.*
23. entent,] entent. *V;* entent *C, A.*
24. Forsakyng] *V;* Forsakyn *C;* Forsaking *A.*   Gods] *C, A;* gods *V.*   leadeth the right] *A;* leadeth right *V;* leadeth ryght *C.*
25. Felowshyp] felowshyp *V, C;* felowship *A.*
26. Abhominable Liuing] abhominable liuing *V;* abhominable lyuing *C, A.*   wholly] *V;* holy *C;* wholy *A.*
27. Good Counsell] good counsell *V;* good counsel *C, A.*   sent] *C, A;* sent, *V.*

55

28. God] *C, A;* god *V.*   forsake] *C, A;* forsake, *V.*
30. Youth] youth *V, C, A.*   Goddes] goddes *V, C;* Gods *A.*
32. Good Councell] good councell *V;* good counsell *C, A.*
33. recitinge] *C;* recistnge *V;* reciting *A.*
35. consolacion] *A;* consolacyon *C;* consolaion *V.*
36. fashion.] fashion *A;* fashiō *C;* fasshiō *V.*
36.1. *SD*] Here entreth lusty Iuuentus or, youth singing as foloweth *V;* Here entreth lusty Iuuentus, or youth singinge as foloweth. *C;* Here entreth lusty Iuuentus, or youth singing as foloweth. *A. SD centered and preceded by paragraph sign in V, C, A. Additional SD Lusty Iuuentus or youth he syngeth V in margin opposite ll. 37-39; omitted C, A.*
37. a slepe] *V;* a slope *C;* a sleepe *A.*
38. the middes] ye middes *V;* the myddes *C, A.*
39. play.] play, *V;* play *C, A.*
41. Me . . . froo] *V;* Me . . . fro *C;* Me thought as I . . . fro *A.*
44. plesure,] plesure: *V;* pleasure, *C, A.*
45. surely pyght] *V, A;* surel ypyght *C.*
46. Of her] *A;* Ofher *V, C.*   sight,] *A;* sight. *V, C.*
48. *Finis.*] Finis. *V, C, A.*
48.1. *SD*] Lusty Iuuentus or youth he speaketh. *V;* Lusty inuentus or youth, he speaketh. *C;* Lusty iuuentus or youth he speaketh. *A centered between ll. 49-50 and preceded by paragraph sign. SD in margin opposite ll. 49-51 in V, C.*
49. *This line omitted in A. Paragraph sign precedes it in V, C.*
55. breake] *V;* brake *C, A.*   the tweche.] *C, A;* ye tweche, *V.*
56. day?] day, *V;* daye *C;* day *A.*
57. game?] game. *V, C, A.*
58. he wyl] *V;* ye wil *C, A.*
61. appetie] *V;* appetyte *C;* appetite *A. The Vele reading seems appropriate to rhyme with* "company" *in line 62.*
63. mynstrell?] mynstrell, *V;* mynstrel, *C;* minstrell, *A.*
65. companions] *V, A;* compacions *C.*   right well] *C, A;* rightwell *V.*
67. me] *V, A;* my *C.*
69.1. *SD*] Here entreth good councel, To whom youth yet speaketh. *in margin opposite ll. 70-73 in V;* Here entreth god counsell. To whō iouth yet speaketh. *in margin opposite ll. 69-73 in C;* Here entreth good counsell. To whom youth he speaketh. *centered after l. 69 and preceded by paragraph sign in A.*

TEXTUAL NOTES

73. wyse] *V;* wyshe *C, A.*
74. them] *A;* thē *V, C.*   whether.] whether *V, C, A.*
75. question] *C, A;* questiō *V.*
81. the time] *A;* ye time *V;* ye tyme *C.*   the scripture] *A;* ye scripture *V;* ye scrypture *C.*
82. agre.] agre, *V, C;* agree. *A.*
85. the vocation] ye vocation *V;* the vocatiō *C, A.*   God] god *V, C, A.*   to.] *A;* to *V;* to, *C.*
87. alone] *C, A;* a lone *V.*   appety] *A;* apety *C;* apetyt *V.*
91. hearinge.] *C;* hearinge, *V;* hearing *A.*
92. God] *A;* god *V, C.*
94. vnmete] *V, C;* not meete *A.*
96. the] ye *V, C, A.*   exhortacion] *A;* exhortaciō *V, C.*
97. Saying] *C, A;* Sayng *V.*
98. encline.] encline *V;* enclyne *C;* enclyne. *A.*
100. counte] coūte *V;* coūt *C;* count *A.*   foole.] foole *V, C, A.*
101. those] *V;* thouse *C;* these *A.*   dyuine] dyuine. *V;* diuine *C;* diuine. *A.*
102. bene] *V, A;* be *C.*
106. in effect] *V, A;* infecte *C.*
109. commaundementes.] cōmaūdemētes *V;* commaūdemēts *C;* commaundements *A.*
112. God] *C, A;* god *V.*
116. God] *C, A;* god *V.*   parcialitie.] *A;* percialitie, *V;* percialitie. *C.*
119. Yea] *V;* Ye *C, A.*   God] *C, A;* god *V.*   with drawe] *C;* withdrawe *A;* with drawe, *V.*
123. he that submitteth] *V, A;* he submetteth *C.*
124. regard,] *A;* regard *V, C.*
127. pray you now] *V;* pray now *C, A.*
128. communicacion] comunicaciō *V;* comunication *C;* communication *A.*   wonders] *V, A;* wondres *C.*   well.] *A;* well *V;* wel *C.*
129. Good Councell.] good councell, *V;* good counsell, *C;* good counsell. *A.*
130. Councell] councell *V;* counsel *C, A.*
131. in fayth] *V, C;* in my fayth *A.*
137. acquaintaunce.] acquaintaunce, *V;* acquayntaunce. *C, A.*
138. God] *C;* god *V, A.*   you] *C, A;* yon *V.*
139. the] ye *V, C, A.*
140. those] *V, C;* these *A.*   Christians] christians *V, C, A.*

142. is so] *C*, *A;* isso *V.*
143. confidence] *C*, *A;* cōfidence *V.*   passyon,] passyon. *V;* passion, *C;* passion *A.*
148. Goddes] goddes *V;* Godds *C;* Gods *A.*   commaundement.] *C*, *A;* commaundement, *V.*
149. expedient] expedient. *V*, *C*, *A.*
151. That] *V*, *C;* that *A.*   Lord] *A;* lord *V;* Lorde *C.*   omnipotente,] *C;* omnipotente. *V;* omnipotent, *A.*
152. To] *V*, *C;* to *A.*
153. most christianly] *C*, *A;* most, christianly *V.*
155.1. SD] *V in margin opposite ll. 156-158;* iuuētus hecuelith *C in margin opposite ll. 156-157;* Iuuentus he kneeleth *A centered between ll. 155-156 and preceded by paragraph sign.*
156. infinite] *C*, *A;* infinitie *V.*
157. of thy] *V*, *A;* of the *C.*
158. with thy spirit] *A;* with spirit *V*, *C.*   continually,] *A;* continually. *V;* continually *C.*
159. may] *V*, *A;* way *C.*
162.1. SD] He riseth *V*, *A;* he riseth. *C. SD in margin opposite line 162 V*, *C*, *A.*
164.1. SD] Knowledg entreth, *V;* knowleg entreth. *C;* Knowledge entreth *A. SD in V*, *C in margin opposite ll. 166-167; in A on line with ch. tag* Good counsell. *between ll. 164-165.* (knowlege entreth. *C*, *Pforzheimer copy.)*
165. (Youth)] (youth) *V;* youth *C*, *A.*   now reioyce] *V*, *C;* now, of whom reioyce *A.*
166. Knowledge of God[s] Veritie] knowledge of god veritie *V;* knowledge of God, verite *C;* knowledge of God, and verity *A.*
170. Ah Good Councell] A good councell *V;* A good counsyl *C;* A good counsel *A.*   now] *V*, *A;* new *C.*
171. God] *A;* god *V*, *C.*
172. Lord] *C*, *A;* lord *V.*   with] *A;* wt *V;* Wt *C.*   benediction] *A;* benedictiō *V;* benedyctyon *C.*
174. the fruition] ye fruitiō *V*, *A;* ye fruityō *C.*
176. Christian] christian *V*, *C*, *A.*
177. Knowlege of Gods Veritie] knowlege of gods veritie *V;* knowledge of gods veritie *C;* knowledg of gods verity *A.*   this mi name] *V;* thus mi name *C;* my nāe *A.*
178. God] *C*, *A;* god *V.*   the] ye, *V*, *C*, *A.*

179. that] *V, C;* the *A.*   Lord] *C, A;* lord *V.*
180. present] *C, A;* presēt *V.*
181. Youth] youth *V, C, A.*
182. Gods pleasure.] *A;* gods pleasure *V;* Gods pleasure *C.*
183. sauiour,] *C, A;* sauiour. *V.*
193. God] *C, A;* god *V.*   decrede.] decrede, *V, C;* decreede, *A.*
195. Lord] *A;* lord *V;* Lorde *C.*
197. recorde] *V;* accorde *C;* accord *A.*
198. .xiii.] *C, A;* .xiii *V.*   psalme] *V, A;* psalmes *C.*
199. O Lord] *A;* O lord *V;* o Lord *C.*
200. thy] *V, A;* the *C.*   precepts] *C, A;* peceptes *V.*
201. Gospell] gospell *V;* Gospel *C, A.*
202. the] ye *V, C, A.*   God] god *V, C, A.*
205. the] ye *V, C, A.*   Galathi,] *V;* Gal, *C;* Gala. *A.*   wryte:] wryte. *V;* wrighte *C;* write *A.*
208. expresse,] *A;* expresse. *V;* expresse *C.*
210. the which it is] *V;* it is *C;* it it is *A.*
211. God] *A;* god *V, C.*   Saint] saint *V, A;* sainct *C.*
215. this is your] *V;* this your *C, A.*
216. when] whē *V, C, A.*   Gods] gods *V, C, A.*   commaundementes] cōmaundementes *V;* commaūdemetes *C;* cōmaūdements *A.*   the] ye *V, C, A.*
221. Goddes] goddes *V, C;* gods *A.*
222. Good] *C, A;* god *V.*
224. Because] *V, A;* Becausy *C.*   Christian] christian *V, C, A.*
228. the .iiii.] ye .iiii. *V, C, A.*
229. Therfore] *V, A;* therfore *C.*
230. from] *C, A;* frō *V.*
232. in him] in hī *V;* in hym *C;* to hym *A.*
234. before.] *C, A;* before, *V.*
236. Saint] saint *V;* sainct *C, A.*
239. cause,] *C, A;* cause. *V.*
240. That] *V, A;* that *C.*
241. Gods] gods *V, C, A.*
243. them] thē *V, C, A.*
245. Lord] *C, A;* lord *V.*
247. To] *V, A;* to *C.*   Gods] *C, A;* gods *V.*
250. thanke the] thāke ye *V, A;* thēke ye *C.*   God] *C, A;* god *V.*   geuen] *C;* geuē *V, A.*   the knowledge] ye knowledge *V, C, A.*

251. the] *C, A;* ye *V.*   peruarte] *V, A;* peruarce *C.*
253. that] *C, A;* yt *V.*   the] *A;* ye *V, C.*
257. owne] *V;* one *C, A.*
262. Christyan] christyan *V;* chrystian *C;* christian *A.*   relygion.] relygion, *V;* religion, *C;* religion. *A.*
263. wisdom] wisdō *V, A;* wysdō *C.*   the wise Salomon] *A;* ye wise Salomō *V;* ye wise Salomon *C.*
264. God] *C, A;* god *V.*   thy] *V, A;* they *C.*
265. then] *A;* thē *V, C.*   promises] *V;* promise *C, A.*   without] wtout *V, C, A.*   exception] *C, A;* exceptiō *V.*
266. them] thē *V, C, A.*   constant] *A;* cōstant *V, C.*
269. assined.] assined *V;* assyned, *C,* assynde. *A.*
270. so kind] *V;* to kynd *C;* to kind *A.*
271. pray you] *V, C;* pray yon *A.*
272. the sixt chapiter of Mathew] *V;* ye vi. chap. Math. *C;* the .vj. chap. Math *A.*
273. done to.] *A;* done to, *V;* done to *C.*
274. God] *C, A;* god *V.*
275. *SD added.*
279. Christian] christian *V, A;* chrystian *C.*
282. which] *V;* that *C, A.*
286. the] ye *V, C, A.*   with] wt *V, A;* Wt *C.*
287. vnfainedly,] *A;* vnfainedly *V;* vnfaynedly *C.*
289. can neuer] *V;* can not neuer *C;* cānot neuer *A.*   tempest.] tempest *V, C, A.*
296. God] *C, A;* god *V.*   do.] do, *V;* do *C, A.*
298. God] *C, A;* god *V.*   to reward] *V;* reward *C, A.*
303. euerlasting] *A;* euerlast *V, C.*
304. leadeth] *V, A;* leadete *C.*
305. brought] *V, A;* borught *C.*
306. worldly] *C, A;* worldy *V.*
308. blesse,] blesse. *V;* blesse *C;* bles, *A.*
309. Good Councell] good councell *V;* good councel *C;* Good counsell *A.*
310. To] *V, A;* to *C.*   this] *V;* his *C, A.*   gospell.] gospell, *V;* Gospel *C, A.*
313. God] *C, A;* god *V.*
317. You] you *V, C, A.*   with] *A;* wt *V;* Wt *C.*   the Lord] *A;* yelord *V;* ye Lord *C.*   pleased.] pleased *V, C, A.*

TEXTUAL NOTES

318. conuersacion] conuersaciō *V, A;* cōuersacion *C.* Youth the Lords] youth ye lords *V;* youth, ye lords *C, A.*
319. season.] ceason, *V;* ceason. *C;* season *A.*   *Exit.*] Exit. *V;* Exit *C, A.*
320. God] *C, A;* god *V.*
321. If] *V;* yf *C;* Yf *A.*   you] *V, A;* thou *C.*   depart,] *C, A;* depart. *V.   Exit.*] Exit *C, A;* exit, *V.*
323. While] *A;* while *V;* Whyle *C.*   world.] *A;* world *V, C.   Exit.*] exit, *V; omitted in C, A.*
323.1. SD]*in margin opposite ll. 324-325 in V, C; centered between ll. 323-324 in A and preceded by paragraph sign.*   Deuill] *V, A;* Deuel *C.   SD and ch. tag added.*
324. *Line preceded by paragraph sign in V.*
327. that] *C, A;* yt *V.*
328. I haue sought] *V, C;* haue I sought *A.*
329. God] *A;* god *V, C.*
333. To] *V, A;* to *C.*   roote] *A;* rote *V, C.*
337. My] *C, A;* my *V.*   deuised.] deuised *V, C, A.*
339. That] *V;* that *C, A.*
340. The] *V;* the *C, A.*   people would] *V;* people woulde *C;* people they would *A.*
342. They] *V;* they *C, A.*
346. To] *V;* to *C, A.*
348. It] *V, A;* yt *C.*
351. That] *V;* that *C. This line omitted in A.*   delight.] delight, *V;* delyght. *C.*
352. taste] *C, A;* tast *V.*   Youth] youth *V, C, A.*
353. Through] *V, A;* through *C.*   Hipocrisie] hipocrisie *V;* hypocrysie *C, A.*
355. That] *V, A;* that *C.*
357. Hipocrisie] hipocrisie *V;* hypocrisie *C;* hipocrisy *A.*
359. sowe.] sowe, *V, C;* sow. *A. This line given to the Deuyl in A; to Hypocrisie in V; ambiguous in C.*
359.1. SD] Here entreth hipocrisye. *in margin opposite ll. 359-360 in V;* Here entreth hypocrysie. *in margin opposite ll. 360-361 in C;* Here entreth Hypocrisy. *centered between ll. 359-360 in A and preceded by paragraph sign.*
363. Whether] *V;* Wether *C;* whether *A.*
364. bochare.] bochare, *V, C;* butchar. *A.*

368. Thou] *V, A;* thou *C.*   deuell.] deuell, *V;* deuell *C;* deuyll, *A.*
369. tel,] tel? *V;* tell? *C;* tell, *A.*
370. am?] *A;* am, *V, C.*
371. Sathan.] *C, A;* Sathan, *V.*
373. You] *V, A;* you *C.*
374. To] *V, A;* to *C.*   vnto] *V, C;* to *A.*
375. why] *C, A;* why. *V.*
376. That] *V, A;* that *C.*
383. You] *V, A;* you *C.*
388. Thou] *V, A;* thou *C.*
393. Gods] *C, A;* gods *V.*
394. awe,] *C, A;* awe. *V.*
395. me.] *C;* me, *V;* mee, *A.*
397. To] *V, A;* to *C.*
399. Gods] *A;* gods *V, C.*
400. intentes] *A;* entēs *V;* intents *C.*
401. That] *V, A;* that *C.*
403. al] *V;* a *Ċ;* all *A.*   Sodometry,] *A;* Sodemetry, *C; omitted V. Lines 403-409 are defective in Vele text where bottom corner of leaf is torn away but leaf mended.*
404. To] *V, A;* to *C.*   mankynde a fall:] *A;* mankynd a fall: *C;* m *V.*
405. brought vp such supersticion] *A;* brought vp suche supersticion *C;* bro *V.*
406. the name of holynes and religion,] *A;* the name of holynes and religyon *C;* the *V̇.*
407. That deceyued almost all.] *A;* that disceyued almoste all. *C;* That disc *V.*
408. holy Cardinals, holy Popes,] *A;* holy Cardinals. holy Popes, *C;* holy *V.*
409. vestimentes, holy copes,] *A;* vestimentes, holy copes *C;* vest *V.*
410. Harmettes] armettes *V;* armytes *C;* Armites *A.*
413. Yea] *V, A;* yea *C.*   obstinate] *V, A;* abstinate *C.*
414. pardons,] *C;* pardons *V;* Pardons, *A.*
417. stockes,] *C, A;* stockes *V.*
418. holy bones] *V, A;* hole bones *C.*
419. Yea] *V, A;* yea *C.*
423. hoodes,] *C, A;* hoodes *V.*
425. And good holy] A good holy *V;* a good holy *C;* And holy *A.*   knaues.] *C, A;* knaues, *V.*

TEXTUAL NOTES

427. twitching] *V, C;* touchings *A.*
429. waxe,] *C, A;* waxe *V.*
431. spirites.] *C, A;* spirites, *V.*
436. Holy knelinge, holy sensynges] knelinge, holy sensynges *V (defective line);* Holy knelynge, holy sensynges *C;* Holy kneling, holy sensynges *A.*
437. *Lines 437-443 are omitted in V; A text given here; C text varies only in sp.:* iouels, myne owne.
446. begune] *V;* begone *C, A.*
450. againe.] againe, *V;* agayne. *C;* agayne, *A.*
451. Youth] youth *V, C;* youths *A.*
453. it is very] *A;* is very *V, C.*
454. That] *V, C;* And that *A.*
457. same.] *C;* same, *V;* same *A.*
460. gospeller?] gospeller, *V;* gospeler. *C;* gospeler? *A.*
462. hath] *V, A;* that *C.*   Good Councel] good councel *V;* good counsell *C, A.*
463. That Knowledge] That knowledge *V;* that knowledge *C, A.*
464. Youth] youth *V, C, A.*
466. But oh] *V;* But ho *C, A.*
467. euer.] euer, *V, C, A.*
469. aduisement.] *C, A;* aduisement, *V.*
472. Knowledge] knowledge *V, C, A.*
474. Gods] *C, A;* gods *V.*   abuse.] abuse, *V, A;* a buse, *C.*
476. To] *V;* to *C, A.*
477. excuse,] *C, A;* excusi. *V.*
478. Those] *V;* those *C, A.*   he] *V;* ye *C, A.*
481. at the bate] *V, C;* at debate *A.*
482. Thou] *V, A;* thou *C.*
483. because] *C, A;* by cause *V.*
484. Thou] *V;* thou *C, A.*   thy] *V, A;* my *C.*   Frendshyp] frendshyp *V, C;* frendship *A.*
486. person.] *A;* person, *V, C.*
488. *Exit.*] Exit. *V; omitted C, A.*
490. Iuuentus] *C, A;* Inuentus *V.*
492. streight,] streight. *V, C;* straight, *A.*
494. snare.] *C;* snare, *V, A.*
500. Yea] *V;* yea *C, A.*
501. Felowship] felowshep *V;* felowshipe *C;* felowship *A.*

TEXTUAL NOTES

505. Lyuyng] lyuyng *V, C;* liuing *A.*
510. Liuinge] liuinge *V;* liuing *C;* lyuing *A.*
511. Yet] *V, A;* yet *C.*
518. Honestie.] honestie, *V;* honestie. *C, A.*
519. Thus] *A;* This *V, C.*
522. Felowship] felowship *V, C, A.*
523. Frendship] frendship *V;* frendshep *C;* friendship *A.*
524. carnally.] *C, A;* carnally, *V.*
525. Hipocrisie] hipocrisie *V;* hypocrysie *C;* hipocrisy *A.*
527. Deuill] deuill *V;* deuel *C;* Deuyll *A.*
530. ful euill] *V;* full euel *C;* euyll *A.*
530.1. SD] Here entreth youth to whom Hypocrisye yet speaketh. *in margin opposite lines 531-535 in V;* Here entreth youth, to whom hepocrysye yet speaketh *in margin opposite ll. 531-535 in C and preceded by paragraph sign;* Youth entreth. *centered between ll. 530-531 in A and preceded by paragraph sign, ch. tag* Hipocrisy *on same line as SD.*
531. Youth] *A;* youth *V, C.*
532. truth] *V;* trouth *C, A.*
533. And] *V, A;* and *C.*
534. You] *V, A;* you *C.*
535. talked] *V;* called *C, A.*
540. dyd abyde] *V;* did a byde *C;* dyd byde *A.*
541. *This line omitted in C and A.*
544. you] *V, C;* ye *A.*
546. were acquainted] *V, C;* were euer acquainted *A.*
548. sone] *V;* some *C;* soone *A.*
549. Youth] youth *V, C, A.*
555. would] *A;* would, *V, C.*
560. You] *V, A;* you *C.*   thus] *A;* this *V, C.*
561. for.] *A;* for *V, C.*
563. Your] *V;* your *C, A.*
567. you] *V, C;* ye *A.*   tender.] *C, A;* tender, *V.*
568. pray you let] *V;* pray let *C;* pray ye let *A.*
569. shew your] *V;* shewe your *C;* shew me your *A.*   nominacion.] *A;* nominacion, *V;* nomination. *C.*
572. Frendshyp] frendshyp *V;* frendship *C, A.*
574. Yet] *V;* yet *C, A.*
575. mastershyp.] mastershyp, *V;* mastership. *C, A.*

TEXTUAL NOTES

576. Frendshyp] frendshyp *V*, *C*; frendship *A*.
577. *Lines 577-579 are given to Juventus in V and C; to Hypocrisie in A.*
579. memory.] memory *V*, *C*, *A*.
583. to go hear a preachinge.] to go hear a preachinge *V*; to go heare a preachyng *C*; to heare a preaching *A*.
584. quod ha] quodha *V*; quod he *C*, *A*.   ah good] *V*; ha good *C*, *A*.
586. instructions] *V*, *A*; instruction *C*.
587. great] *V*, *C*; greatly *A*.
589. shew not] *V*, *C*; shewe me *A*.
590. fantesies.] *A*; fantesies: *V*; fantesies *C*.
592. You] *V*, *A*; you *C*.
594. for those] *V*; for al those *C*, *A*.
595. communycacyon.] *C*; communycacyon *V*; communication. *A*.
598-599. *Ch. tag* iuuetus *misplaced opposite l. 600, ch. tag* Hipocrysye *omitted, making ll. 598-599 seem to be spoken by Hipocrisye and ll. 600-609 by Juventus in C.*
602. can.] *A*; can, *V*; can *C*.
604. Gods] *C*, *A*; gods *V*.
605. Christen] chisten *V*, *C*, *A*.
615. Youth] youth *V*, *C*, *A*.
616. Sir Iohn] sir Ihon *V*; syr Ihon *C*; syr Iohn *A*.
617. for you to] *V*; for to *C*; for such as you to *A*.
618. You] *V*, *C*; you *A*.   Gods] *C*, *A*; gods *V*.   testament.] *A*; testament, *V*; testamēt *C*.
627. worde.] *C*; worde, *V*; word *A*.
628. Whether] *V*; whether *C*, *A*.
629. Goddes] *C*; goddes *V*; Gods *A*.
630. thynke] *A*; thike *V*; thynge *C*.   the . . . the] *C*, *A*; ye . . . ye *V*.
632. opinion] *A*; opion *V*, *C*.
635. taught] *V*, *A*; thought *C*.   sort, of people] *V*; sort of the people *C*, *A*.
638. You] *V*; you *C*, *A*.
639. were] *C*, *A*; where *V*.
644. obedient?] *A*; obedient. *V*; obedient *C*.
646. lawfull.] lawfull? *V*; lawful? *C*; lawful *A*.
647. quod ha] *C*, *A*; quodha *V*.
648. Wylt] *V*; Wil *C*; Wilt *A*.
649. When] *V*, *C*; when *A*.
656. foule] *V*, *A*; foole *C*.   presumption] *V*; presumptious *C*; pre-

sumptions *A*.
657. Wyl] *V;* wyll *C, A*.
661. God] *C, A;* god *V*.
664. Goddes] goddes *V;* godds *C;* gods *A*.
665. was.] *C;* was *V;* was, *A*.
668. What] *V, C;* what *A*.
669. I wote] *V, A;* I wote wote *C*.
670. We] *V, C;* we *A*.
671. Yea] *V;* yea *C, A*.   to.] to, *V, A;* to *C*.
675. I should] *V;* I would *C, A*.   vse,] *A;* vse. *V, C*.
677. What] *V, A;* what *C*.
685. cloynes of the plough] *A;* ioynyng of ye plough *V;* ioynyng of the plough *C*.
686. face] *V;* fare *C, A*.
690. Yonder] *V, A;* yonder *C*.
692. so beate] *V;* beare *C, A*.
693. That] *V, A;* that *C*.
694. That] *V, A;* that *C*.
695. meryly] *C;* merely *V, A*.
696. best.] *C;* best, *V, A*.
698. Will] *V, C;* will *A*.
702. That] *V;* that *C, A*.
703. puruyes] *V;* purures *C;* puruies *A*.
704. commynge] *C;* commyuge *V;* comming *A*.
705. iybbere] *A;* Iybberd *V;* fybbere *C*.
706. We] *V;* we *C, A*.
708. We] *V, A;* we *C*.
710. You] *V, A;* you *C*.   with] *A;* wt *V;* Wt *C*.
711. you] *V, C;* yon *A*.   see my cunnyng] *V;* see cunnyng *C;* see cunning *A*.
712. a liuinge] aliuinge *V;* aliuing *C;* a liuing *A*.
713. amongest] *C;* A mongest *V, A*.
713.1. SD] Here entreth *in margin opposite lines 714-715, and ch. tag* felowshyp *opposite line 716 in V; opposite line 712, and ch. tag* Felowshyp *opposite lines 718-719 in C; omitted, and ch. tag centered in A.   Additional SD added.*
715. purse,] *C, A;* purse. *V*.
716. this.] *A;* this, *V;* thys *C*.
717. Frendshyp] frendshyp *V, C;* frendship *A*.

719. his promis] *V;* thys promys *C;* this promis *A.*
720. mine.] *A;* mine, *V;* mine *C.*
720.1. *SD added.*
721. Yes] *V, A;* yes *C.*   Felowshyp] felowshyp *V, C;* felowship *A.*
722. hour] *V;* oure *C;* houre *A.*
724. *Ch. tag* felowshyp *opposite l. 724 V; opposite ll. 724-725 C;* Felowship *centered between ll. 723-724 in A, obviously an error since l. 724 is Hypocrisie's.*
725. wylt] *V;* will *C;* wil *A.*
726. Frendshyp] frendshyp *V, C;* frendship *A.*
727. be.] *A;* be, *V;* be *C.*
728. God] *C, A;* god *V.*
730. syrra] *V, C;* sir *A.*
731. he is] *V, C;* he his *A.*
735. on] *A;* in *V, C.*
736. nones.] *C, A;* nones, *V.*
737. dogs] *V;* gods *C, A.*
738. You] *V, A;* you *C.*   *SD added.*
741. You *V;* you *C, A.*   lye,] *C, A;* lye. *V.*
743. mynde.] *C;* mynde *V;* mind. *A.*
745. kindnes.] kindnes *V;* kyndnes *C;* kindnes, *A.*
746. gentelmans] *A;* gentylman *V;* gentelman *C.*   fynes] *V, C;* fynenes *A.*
747. Your] *V;* your *C, A.*
749. were] *V;* wery *C, A.*
751. God] *C, A;* god *V.*
752. Felowshyp] felowshyp *V;* felowship *C, A.*
753. you se] *V, C;* you not see *A.*   Besse] besse *V, C, A.*
755. afrayd.] afrayd, *V;* afraid. *C, A.*
758. goes] goeth *V, C, A.*
760. the] *C, A;* ye *V.*   preching.] preching *V;* preachynge *C;* preaching *A.*
766. vs to be] *V;* vs be *C, A.*   no.] no, *V;* no *C, A.*
768. with] wt *V, A;* Wt *C.*   that] *V;* a *C, A.*   can] cā *V, C, A.*
769. a one] *V;* one *C, A.*   with] *A;* wt *V;* Wt *C.*   meat.] meat, *V;* meate, *C, A.*
771. be gone.] be gone, *V;* be gone *C;* begon *A.*
772. come for vs her] *V;* com her *C, A.*
777. Yea] *V, A;* yea *C.*   with] wt *V, A;* Wt *C.*

68 TEXTUAL NOTES

779.   You] *V, A;* you *C.*
781.   thinke it] *V;* thynketh *C;* thinketh *A.*
784.   Yea] *V, A;* yea *C.*   Gods] *C, A;* gods *V.*   *No ch. tag to show that ll. 784-785 belong to Juventus, V, C. Ch. tag* Iuuentus *preceded by paragraph sign in margin opposite l. 783 instead of being centered as usual in A.*
785.   secretly.] secretly *V, C, A.*
785.1. *SD added.*
786.   Hem,] *C, A;* Hem. *V.*
787.   open] *V;* opned *C;* opened *A.*
788.   Felowship] felowship *V, C, A.*   waye.] *C, A;* waye *V.*
789.   Unknowen Honestie] vnknowen honestie *V;* vnknowne honestye *C;* vnknowne honesty *A.*   [I pray]] *supplied to rhyme with* waye *in l. 788.*
790.   You] *V, A;* you *C.*   God] *C, A;* god *V.*
791.   you nede not] *V, C;* you not *A.*
792.   yonge gentylman] *V;* yong gentelman *C;* gentelman *A.*   here.] here, *V, C, A.*
797.   thynke] *V;* thyng *C;* thinke *A.*
798.   Yf] *V;* yf *C;* If *A.*   goulde.] goulde, *V, C;* gold. *A.*
799.   Yes] *V, A;* yes *C.*
800.   smocke.] *A;* smocke, *V;* smocke *C.*
803.   That] *C, A;* that *V.*   wantons company] wātōs cōpany *V;* wātōs cōpani *C;* wātons company *A.*   myne.] myne *V, C, A.*
804.   dogs] *V, C, A.*   that] yt *V, C, A.*   whorson villain] whorsō villaī *V;* horson vyllain *C;* horson villain *A.*
805.   do me] *V;* dome *C;* do we *A.*
806.   gogs] *V, A;* gods *C.*
808.   masse.] masse, *V;* masse *C;* mas. *A.*
810.   That] *V, C;* that *A.*   loue.] *A;* loue, *V;* loue *C.*
812.   litle] *C, A;* lile *V.*
816.   that.] *C, A;* that, *V.*
816.1. *SD]* Iuuentus kisseth abhominable liuing. *centered and preceded by paragraph sign in A;* Iuuentus he kisseth. *in margin opposite ll. 816-817 in V;* iuuētus kisseth. *in margin opposite ll. 817-818 in C. SD serves also as ch. tag in V, C, A.*
818.   You] *V, A;* you *C.*   to] *V, C;* into *A.*
823.   You] *V, A;* you *C.*   will] *V;* well *C;* would *A.*
824.   If you] *V, A;* yf thou *C.*

TEXTUAL NOTES

828. tune.] *C*, *A;* tune, *V.*
829. What] *V*, *A;* what *C.*
830. company] *C*, *A;* compauy *V.*
832. if it] *C*, *A;* ifit *V.*
833. sure.] *C*, *A;* sure, *V.*
835. Frendshyp] frendshyp *V, C;* friendship *A.*   goeth] *A;* goth *V, C.*
836. conceite.] *A;* conceite, *V;* conceyte *C.*
837. quod ha] *C;* quodha *V;* quoth ha *A.*
838. wel saye she] *V;* welsay that she *C;* well say that she *A.*
839. Unknowen Honestie] vnknowen honestie *V;* vnknowne honestie *C;* vnknowen honestye *A.*
840. Felowship] felowship *V;* felowshyp *C;* fellowship *A.*
841. Ye] *V;* ye *C;* Yes *A.*
843. Youth] youth *V, C, A.*
843.1. SD] he kisseth *in margin below ch. tag* Iuuentus *opposite l. 846 in V;* he kysseth *in margin opposite l. 844 below ch. tag* iuuētus *in C; SD omitted in A.*
844. pleasunt] plesaũt *V;* pleasūt *C;* pleasant *A.*
846. with] wt *V, A;* Wt *C.*   hence.] *C;* hence *V, A.*
848. bene.] *A;* bene, *V;* bene *C.*
849. What] *V, A;* what *C.*   is] *V;* where *C;* were *A.*   deadly synne] *V;* daly synne *C;* dayly synne *A.*
851. bare.] *C, A;* bare, *V.*
852. much fye] *V;* much fie *C;* a mischiefe *A.*   baudy] *V, A;* badi *C.*   you] *V, C;* ye *A.*
853. wysse] *A;* wosse *V, C.*   Frendship] frendship *V, C;* frenship *A.*   mought] *V, A;* mouth *C.*
854. What] *V, A;* what *C.*   that the] yt the *V;* ye *C, A.*   surmise.] surmise *V, C, A.*
857. sword.] *C;* sword *V;* sworde. *A.*
858. Gods] gods *V, C, A.*
859. fyghte.] fyghte, *V;* fight *C;* fight. *A.*
865. Your] *V, A;* your *C.*
867. a blowe] *C, A;* ablowe *V.*
871. You] *V, A;* you *C.*   inough] *A;* Inongh *V;* ynough *A.*   all.] *A;* all, *V, C.*
875. It] *V, A;* yt *C.*
876. me and if] *V;* me, and yf *C;* me, if *A.*
877. will] *V;* shall *C;* wyll *A.*

880. thre.] thre, *V, C;* three. *A.*
883. eare] *V, C;* euer *A.*
883.1. *SD*] They synge as foloweth *in margin opposite ll. 884-885 in V;* The sing as foloweth, *in margin opposite ll. 884-885 in C;* They sing as foloweth. *centered between ll. 883-884 in A and preceded by paragraph sign.*
887. you.] *C, A;* you, *V.*
889. month of Maye] *V;* month Maye *C;* month of May *A.*
890. fayd] *V, C;* vade *A.*
891. you.] *C, A;* you, *V.*
892. bare?] *A;* bare, *V, C.*
895. you.] *C, A;* you *V.*
897. hys] *V;* thys *C;* this *A.*
899. you.] *C, A;* you, *V.*
899.1. *SD*] They go furth, *in margin opposite ll. 900-901 in V;* They go fourth. *in margin opposite l. 900 in C;* They go fourth. *centered between 899-900 in A but not preceded by paragraph sign as usual.*
901. bynde,] bynde, &c. *V;* bynde. &c. *C, A.*
902-903. *Inserted here from ll. 886-887 of Vele text. SD added.*
903.1. *SD*]Here entreth good councell. *in margin opposite ll. 902-903 in V;* Here entreth god counsell. *in margin opposite ll. 901-903 in C;* Here entreth Good counsell. *centered between ll. 901-902 in A and preceded by paragraph sign. SD also serves as ch. tag in V, C, A.*
904. Lord] *C, A;* lord *V.*   cease] *A;* seace *V, C.*
906. Youth] youth *V, C, A.*   & testament] *omitted C.*
907. Abhominable Liuinge] abhominable liuinge *V;* abhominable lyuyng *C;* abominable lyuing *A.*
908. professyng] *V;* profession *C, A.*
910. confusion.] *A;* confusion, *V;* confusyon. *C.*
911. is now] *V;* is *C, A.*
912. professors] *A;* professour *V, C.*
913. congregation] cōgregatiō *V; omitted C;* & trusty *A.*
915. vtterly abhored?] vtterly abhored, *V;* abhord vtterly *C;* abhord vtterly? *A.*
917. We] *V, A;* we *C.*
918. the] *C, A;* ye *V.*   longe] *C;* lōge *V;* long *A.*
919. Which] *V, A;* wich *C.*   Gods] *C, A;* gods *V.*   spirit?] *A;* spirit, *V, C.*

920. With] *V, A;* with *C.*
922. Who] *V, A;* who *C.*
923. vnto] *V, C;* to *A.*
924. there be now but a fewe] *A;* few that liue now *V;* few that lyue nowe *C.*
925. the] *A;* ye *V, C.* example] *A;* exāple *V, C.*
927. wickedly] *V, A;* wicked *C.*
928. God] *C, A;* god *V.*
930. Lord] *A;* lord *V;* Lorde *C.*
933. Youth] youth *V, C, A.* Gods] *C, A;* gods *V.*
934. Knowledge] knowledge *V, C, A.*
935. instructions] *V;* instructiō *C;* instruction *A.*
938.1. *SD*] Here entreth Iuuentus *in margin opposite ll. 936-939 in V;* Her entreth Iuuentus *in margin opposite ll. 937-938 in C;* Here entreth Iuuentus. *centered between ll. 938-939 in A and preceded by paragraph sign. SD also serves as ch. tag in V, C, A.*
940. sice] *V;* cyce *C, A.*
942. come.] come: *V, C, A.*
943. Youth, Youth] youth, youth *V;* youth youth *C, A.*
945. Gods] *C, A;* gods *V.*
947. Capernite] capernite *V, C, A.*
949. Abhominable Liuinge] abhominable liuinge *V;* abhomynable lyuynge *C;* abhominable ltuing *A.*
950. What] *V, A;* what *C.*
951. spyrt,] *C, A;* spyrt. *V.*
952. not a] *V, A;* a *C.*
953. What] *V, A;* what *C.* lose] *C;* losi *V;* loose *A.*
956. shift] *V, A;* shyfe *C.* men.] *C, A;* men, *V.*
958. Knowledge] knowledge *V, C, A.*
959. You] *V, A;* you *C.*
960. Gods] *C, A;* gods *V.*
962. verytie] *C;* viritie *V;* veryty *A.* God] *C, A;* god *V.*
964. Your] *V, A;* you *C.*
965. You] *V, A;* you *C.*
966. eies.] eies, *V;* eyes, *C;* eyes. *A.*
967. Deuil] deuil *V;* deuell *C, A.* the] ye *V, C, A.*
968. trapt] *V;* trape *C, A.* in] *V, C;* id *A.* Hypocrisye] hypocrisye *V;* hypocrye *C;* hipocrysy *A.*

TEXTUAL NOTES

971. thus] *A;* this *V;* thys *C.*   reproue] *V;* report *C, A.*
973. Your] *V, A;* your *C.*
975. my mind.] my mind *V;* my mynde *C;* me mind *A.*
977. agayne.] *C, A;* agayne, *V.*
978. complayne] *V, A;* complaye *C.*
979. you] *V;* ye *C, A.*   Christes] *A;* christes *V;* Chrystes *C.*
982. Who] *V, A;* who *C.*
984. Yea] *V, A;* yea *C.*
986. will?] will *V;* wyll *C;* wyll? *A.*
987. What] *V;* what *C, A.*
989. S. Paul] *C, A;* S, Paul *V.*
991. Christians name.] *A;* christians name, *V;* christians name. *C.*
992. you] *V, C;* ye *A.*
994. your most] *V, A;* our most *C.*
995. do] *V, C;* do not *A.*
997. communicacion] *V;* communycacyon *C;* abomination *A.*
998. Youth] youth *V, C, A.*
1000. Youth] youth *V, C, A.*
1001. aduaunce] *A;* auaunce *V, C.*
1002. ye] *V, C;* you *A.*
1003. this blaspheming] *V;* thys plasphemyng *C;* thus blaspheming *A.*
1004. what] *C, A;* what. *V.*   S. Paul] S, Paul *V;* saynt, Paule *C;* Saynt Paule *A.*
1007. knowledge] *C, A;* knowldge *V.*
1008. looking] *A;* lokīg *V, C.*
1009. And] *V, C;* & *A.*   terrible] *V, A;* tribble *C.*   which] *V;* whych *C;* yt *A.*
1013. haue I] *V, A;* I haue *C.*
1015. late.] *A;* late, *V;* late *C.*
1015.1. SD] He lyeth downe. *in margin opposite l. 1015 in V;* He lyeth douu, *in margin opposite ll. 1015-1016 in C;* Here Iuuentus lyeth downe. *centered between ll. 1015-1016 in A and preceded by paragraph sign.*
1017. God] *C, A;* god *V.*   wold] *V;* wolde *C;* would *A.*
1018. this] *C, A;* his *V.*
1019. iustly] *V, A;* iusty *C.*
1021. my owne] *V, C;* myne own *A.*
1023. Youth] youth *V, C, A.*
1024. thin] *V;* thine *C;* thy *A.*

TEXTUAL NOTES   73

1025.   condempnation] *C;* condepnation *V;* condempnatiō *A.*
1026.   Yet] *V, A;* yet *C.*   God] *C, A;* god *V.*
1027.   surmise?] *C, A;* surmise: *V.*
1028.   Thinkest you not] *A;* Thinkest not *V;* Thinckest not *C.*   Gods] *C, A;* gods *V.*
1029.   comfort] *A;* cōfort *V, C.*   him.] *A;* him *V;* hi *C.*
1032.   God] god *V, C, A.*
1033.   created.] *C, A;* created, *V.*
1034.   Ah] A *V, C, A.*
1035.   God] *A;* god *V, C.*
1039.   remembre.] remembre, *V;* remembre *C;* remember *A.*
1040.   lenger] *V, C;* longer *A.*
1041.   Lord] *A;* lord *V;* Lorde *C.*
1044.   mynde.] *A;* mynde, *V, C.*
1045.   God] *C, A;* god *V.*
1046.1. *SD*] Here entreth gods mercyeull promyses, *in margin opposite ll. 1047-1049 in V;* Here entreth goddes merciful promises. *in margin opposite ll. 1048-1051 in C;* Here entreth Gods mercifull promises. *centered between ll. 1047-1048 in A and preceded by paragraph sign.*
1047.1. *Ch. tag added.*
1048.   Lorde] lorde *V;* Lord *C, A.*
1054.   Lord] *C, A;* lord *V.*
1056.   Saint] saint *V, A;* sainct *C.*
1056.1. *Ch. tag*] Gods merciful promi *V.*
1057.   Yes] *V, A;* yes *C.*   them] thē *V, C, A.*
1058.   Saint Paul] saint paul *V;* sainct Paul *C;* saint Paul *A.*   the] ye *V, C, A.*   by vyolence] byvyolēce *V;* by violēce *C, A.*
1060.   Thus] *A;* thus *C;* This *V.*   Saint Augustine] saint Augustine *V;* sainct Austine *C;* sainct Austine *A.*
1061.   If] *V;* yf *C;* Yf *A.*   Lordes] *C, A;* lordes *V.*
1063.   This] *V, A;* this *C.*
1064.   Shal be] *V;* Salbe *C;* Shalbe *A.*
1066.   That] *V, A;* that *C.*
1066.1. *SD*] He riseth Iuuentus *in margin opposite ll. 1068-1070 in V;* Her riseth Iuuentus *in margin opposite ll. 1068-1069 in C;* Here riseth Iuuentus. *centered between ll. 1067-1068 in A and preceded by paragraph sign. SD also serves as ch. tag in V, C, A.*
1068.   These] *V, A;* these *C.*

1069. To] *V*, *A*; to *C*.   place.] *C*, *A*; place *V*.
1070. obtayne] *A*; optayne *V*, *C*.
1072. alone] *C*, *A*; alone. *V*.
1074. Therfore] *V*; therfore *C*; Therefore *A*.
1076. praysed.] *C*; praysed, *V*; praised. *A*.
1078. Which] *V*; which *C*, *A*.   goodes] *V*; good *C*, *A*.   doth] *V*; dooth *C*; had *A*.
1081. Wherfore] *V*; wherfore *C*, *A*.
1082. was] *V*, *A*; as *C*.
1083. returned] *V*, *A*; returnen *C*.
1086. Brode] *C*, *A*; Borde *V*.
1087. life ful] lifeful *V*; lyfe, full *C*; life, full *A*.
1088. He] *V*, *A*; he *C*.   Gods spyrite] Godsspyrite *V*, *C*; Gods spirit *A*.
1089. And] *V*, *A*; and *C*.
1090. Although] *V*, *A*; although *C*.   neuer so] *C*, *A*; neuerso *V*.   Gods] *C*, *A*; gods *V*.   word.] word *V*, *C*, *A*.
1092. falshed] *V*, *C*; falshod *A*.
1094. not] *C*, *A*; mot *V*.
1095. one in the world] *V*, *A*; on the world *C*.
1097. bayte.] bayte *V*; bayt *C*; baite *A*.   to] *V*, *C*; so *A*.
1098. Christyanly] christyanly *V*; christianly *C*, *A*.
1099. Knowledge] knowled *V*; knowledg *C*; knowledge *A*.   Good Councell] good councell *V*; good councel *C*; good counsell *A*.
1101. the] *C*, *A*; ye *V*.
1103. peruert] *V*, *C*; peruart *A*.
1104. from] *A*; frō *V*, *C*.   ye] ẙ *V*, *C*, *A*; *usually* ye *meaning* you *is spelled out.*   hert.] *V*; hart *C*, *A*.
1105. Hipocrisie] hipocrisie *V*; hypocrysie *C*; hipocrisy *A*.
1107. desyres] *V*; desyre *C*; desire *A*.
1108. on it] *V*; of it *C*, *A*.   doth yet] *V*; doth *C*, *A*.
1109. the title] *V*; the tytle *C*; tytle *A*.   Frendshyp] frendshyp *V*, *C*; frendship *A*.
1110. Felowship] felowship *V*, *A*; feloshyp *C*.
1111. Abhominable Liuyng.] abhominable liuyng, *V*; abhominable lyuing *C*; abhominable liuing. *A*.
1114. Good Councel] good councel *V*; good counsell *C*, *A*.
1116. Christian] *A*; christian *V*; Christan *C*.
1117. the] *C*, *A*; ye *V*.
1118. same.] *C*; same *V*; same, *A*.

TEXTUAL NOTES

1119. Yet] *V, A;* yet *C.*   God] *C, A;* god *V.*   mercy] *C, A;* mercy. *V.*
1126. All Christen] *C, A;* sten *V; first part of ll. 1126-1128 is torn away in V, but leaf mended.*
1126.1. SD added.
1127. May learne] *C, A;* rn *V.*   Hipocrise] hipocrise *V;* hypocrysye *C;* hipocrysy *A.*
1128. With the which] *C, A;* which *V.*   Deuil] deuil *V;* deuel *C;* deuill *A.*   with] wt *V;* Wt *C, A.*
1131. them] *A;* thē *V, C.*   with Gods] wt gods *V;* Wt Gods *C;* wt Gods *A.*
1132. disceiueth] *V;* deceued *C, A.*   trust.] *A;* trust *V, C.*
1133. Frendshyp] frēdshyp *V;* frēdship *C;* frendship *A.*
1134. Gods] *C, A;* gods *V.*
1135. ye] *V;* you *C, A.*
1136. the] *C;* ye *V, A.*   doings] *V, C;* doing *A.*
1137. Kinred nor Felowship] kinred nor felowship *V;* kynred nor felowshyp *C;* kindred nor felowship *A.*
1139. then] thē *V, C, A.*   audite.] audite *V, C, A.*
1141. testament] *C;* testamēt *V, A.*
1142. If] *V, A;* yf *C.*
1143. Gods] *C;* gods *V, A.*
1145. And] *V, A;* & *C.*   don] dō *V;* dū *C;* done *A.*
1146. Your] *V;* youre *C;* your *A.*
1147. Say] *V, C;* say *A.*   long] *C, A;* lōg *V.*   shortened] shor tened *V;* shortēed *C;* shortēd *A.*
1148. the] ye *V, C, A.*   toies] *V;* ioyes *C, A.*
1149. For] *V, C;* for *A.*
1151. For] *V, C;* for *A.*   with] wt *V, A;* Wt *C.*   Lords] lords *V, A;* lordes *C.*   coming] cōming *V, A;* cōmīg *C.*   sodenli] sodēli *V;* sodēly *C;* sodenly *A.*
1153. bi] *V;* be *C, A.*   the] *C;* ye *V, A.*
1155. the] *V;* ye *C, A.*   king] *V;* quene *C, A.*
1156. his] *V;* her *C, A.*   he] *V;* she *C, A.*
1157. God] *C;* god *V, A.*
1158. Lord] *C, A;* lord *V.*   his] *V;* her *C, A.*
1159. him] *V;* her *C, A.*
1160. his] *V;* her *C, A.*   captayne.] c *V;* seruant. *C;* seruaunt. *A; ll. 1160-1163 are partially torn away in V, but leaf mended.*
1161. vs pray] *V, A;* vs for *C.*   this realme,] *A;* this *V;* this realme *C.*

TEXTUAL NOTES

1162.   his] is *V;* her *C, A.*   auctorised,] *C, A;* au *V.*
1164.   his] *V, C, A.*
1165.   that they] *V;* they *C, A.*
1167.   seke] *V;* sesse *C, A.*   redrest.] *C, A;* redrest, *V.*
1169.   God] *C, A;* god *V.*
1170.1. *Finis.*] Finis. *V, A;* Finis *C.*   quod] *V;* Quod *C, A.*
Colophon] Imprynted at London, in Lothbury, ouer agaynst Sainct Margarits Church, by Wyllyam Copland. *(Preceded by paragraph sign.) (C)*
Imprinted at London by Iohn Awdely dwelling in little Britayne strete without Aldersgate. *(A)*

Glosses

Prologue] The first fourteen lines of the Prologue follow closely the apocryphal book of Ecclesiasticus, Chapter 30, though the first two lines have their basis in Genesis 8.21 ("And the Lorde say de [sic] in hys herte: I wyll not proceade to cursse the grou nde [sic] any more for mannes sake, for the ymaginacyon of manes hert is euel euen from his youth. . . .") and Jeremiah 17.8 ("Amonge all thinges man hathe the mooste dysceytfull and stubburne herte.").

3-7.] Ecclesiasticus Ch. 30: "Who so loueth his chylde holdeth him styl vnder correctiō that he may haue ioye of him afterwarde . . . He that teacheth his son, shall haue ioye of hym . . . Who so enfourmeth and teacheth his sonne, greueth the enemye: and before his frendes he may haue ioye of hym. . . . An vntamed horse wyll be harde, and a wantō child wyll be wylfull. . . ."

8-10.] Ecclesiasticus Ch. 30: "Gyue hym no lybertie in his youth, and excuse not his folye. Bowe downe his necke whyle he is younge, hyt hym vpon the sydes, whyle he is yet but a childe, lest he waxe stubburne, and gyue nomore force of the, & so shalt thou haue heuynesse of soule. Teach thy child and be dyligent therin, lest it be to thy shame. . . ."

Quotations are from The Byble in Englysh, that is to saye the content of all the holy scrypture, both of the olde and newe Testament with a Prologe thereinto [sic], made by the reuerende father in God, Thomas archebyshop of Cantorbury. This is the Byble appoynted to the vse of ye churches. Prynted by Edwarde Whitchurch. *Cum priuilegio ad imprimendum solum.* Finished the .xxviii. daye of Maye, Anno Domini M.D.XLI.

37. Cf. opening of *Piers Plowman.*
45. pyght] smitten; cf. Chaucer, "He pighte hym on the pomel of his heed," The Knight's Tale, 2689.
53. passe] care.
55. the touch] in touch.
85. vocation] a call or invitation given by God to the Christian life or to some particular service or profession.
95. Ephesians 5.15-16.
104. Deuteronomy 29.9-13.
140. Revelation 14.4.
205. Galatians 5.22-23.

GLOSSES

213. Romans 14.23.
220. See Introduction for a discussion of justification by faith and works.
236. conuersations] manner of living, conduct, or behavior: "All are banish'd till their conversations / Appear more wise and modest to the world," Shakespeare, *2 Henry IV*, V. v. 100-101.
236-237. I Peter 1.18.
243. Refers to Roman or Pope Catholics.
256-260. Juventus' parents were evidently Roman or Pope Catholics.
263. Psalms 111.10.
267-269. Luke 10.27 and Matthew 22.37-39.
283-284. Perhaps Matthew 5.11?
286. Perhaps an echo of Matthew 16.18?
292. conuersacion] see note above, l. 236.
302. imagination] a scheme, plotting or devising evil.
304. conuersation] see note above, l. 236.
325. geare] business or affair.
327. policie] cunning contrivance, stratagem, trick.
340. Refers to Roman or Pope Catholics.
352. taste] to test, try, prove: "And taste it wel and stoon thou shalt it fynde," Chaucer, Second Nun's Tale, 503.
359. kepe agayne] keep back, as in "againask" meaning "ask back"; or "againbuy" meaning "buy back" or "redeem."
364. bochare] butcher: John Bale called the Pope a "bloudy bocher," *King Johan*, l. 2407.
368. chapman] merchant, dealer, trader.
388. not benne worthe a flaunders pin] proverb; cf. Thomas Ingelend, *Disobedient Child*, "Or els all is not worth a Brasse pynne," Tilley, *Dictionary of Proverbs*.
403. Sodometry] suggested as resulting from state of celibacy required of Catholic priests.
409. copes] a large capelike vestment worn by priests in certain religious ceremonies.
410. Harmettes] hermits.
418. cloughtes] pieces of cloth.
420. skinnes] parchment.   bulles] papal letters written on parchment.
421. Rochettes] a close-fitting linen vestment resembling the surplice, but having close sleeves reaching to the hands, worn by bishops and abbots in certain ceremonies.   coules] cowls, monks' hoods.
422. crouches and staues] ceremonial bendings and pastoral staffs of

GLOSSES

bishop or abbot, being the symbol of his office as a shepherd of the flock of God.

424. Miters] miter, a bishop's official headdress having a cleft top.

429. holy waxe, holy leade] wax used to seal papal bulls; lead used for a round seal attached to papal bulls, having representation of St. Peter on one side and name of Pope using it on the other.

430-431. Using holy water and holy bread for superstitious purposes such as driving away evil spirits from one's house was forbidden by royal proclamations in the reign of Henry VIII.

432. holy fyre, holy palme] burning incense used in the censers at religious ceremonies; branch of palm tree carried the Sunday before Easter commemorating Christ's triumphal entry into Jerusalem when the multitude strewed palm branches in the way.

433. Holy oyle, holy creame] chrism: oil, usually mixed with balm or balm and spices, consecrated by the bishop on Maundy Thursday, and used in the administration of sacraments.

434. holy asshes] holy ashes, put on heads of penitents on Ash Wednesday, the first day of Lent.

436. sensynges] perfumings with burning incense.

438. Holy crosses, holy belles] cruciform badge, ornament, or article of ecclesiastical furniture, as a staff carried in religious processions; bells sounded during mass to guard against evil spirits.

443. A blasphemous suggestion paralleling himself, son of Satan, to Christ, son of God.

451. Gods word] The Bible in English translation was first authorized in England in 1537 and 1539 by Henry VIII, who ordered a copy placed in all churches.

460. newe gospeller] a satiric term applied to those reformers who emphasized a personal, individualized, literal interpretation of the New Testament.

470. incontinent] immediately.

476-478. Hypocrisie will persuade Juventus to abuse God's word, an activity at which he has always been good. He will also make excuses for these sinful activities which the reformed Juventus now abjures.

481. at the bate] beaten down, wasted away. The other two sixteenth-century texts read "at debate," meaning "under debate."

495. geare] business, affair.

499. conuersation] see note above, l. 236.

507. tyse] entice.

GLOSSES

513. procure] to pimp, obtain for illicit intercourse or prostitution.
524. carnally] lustfully or sensually.
530. Note the irony here: the Devil's evil will be to punish his son.
537. Me thought] it seemed to me.
541. tyde] time.
556. straunge] reserved, distant.
560. to calenge] to challenge, accuse, or blame.
565. wisse] know.
569. nominacion] name.
583. preachinge] sermon.
584. preaching] a slang term for sexual encounter.
585. wynnyng] encounter.
592. spyrt] spurt.
601. Does Hypocrisie mean that the preacher will merely state the obvious? Shakespeare has Dogberry use "God's a good man" as a mild oath in *Much Ado About Nothing*, III. v. 39.
616. portous] an abbreviated Mass Book. Sir Iohn] traditional name for a priest.
618. Gods testament] the New Testament.
625. to make a burne] to be burned for heresy.
628. a halter or a corde] to be hanged or tied to the stake.
629. Goddes mother] the Virgin Mary.
640. infidelitie] holding false beliefs.
655. preaty geare] pretty state of affairs.
666. For once do not pass up the chance to break a promise.
669. wote] know.
675. peraduenture] perhaps.
680. Do what your own lust] do your own pleasure.
681. affinitie] companionship or acquaintance.
682. Luke 6.42.
685. cloynes] clowns (country bumpkins).
687. gyrdle] belt.
693. flusshe] flushed out.
698. pye feast] meat pie feast, perhaps steak or kidney pie.
701. furny carde] a procuress.
703. She puruyes] she provides for me, with suggestion of sexual favors.
705. iybbere] gibber, to chatter unintelligibly, to utter gibberish.
708. puddinge] a piece of intestine stuffed with seasoned chopped meat

GLOSSES 81

or the like and boiled.
719. beshrew] curse.
729. mary bone] marrow bone.
736. for the nones] for the present occasion, a complimentary remark here.
737. dogs precious bones] a euphemized oath.
739. I desire to know you better.
746. fynes] fine manners, a sarcastic remark.
753. Besse] short for Elizabeth; a generic term for a girl, here specifically referring to Abhominable Liuing.
754. yester night] last night.
767. go] walk.
772. anone] presently.
774. becke] beckon.
775. gallaunde] high-spirited girl, with a sexual connotation.
791. to fraie] to be afraid, to fear.
800. smocke] chemise: loose undergarment or slip.
804-808. The first two oaths in this stanza are euphemized (as in Shakespeare's "by gogs-wouns" in *The Taming of the Shrew*, III. ii. 162). Juventus' swearing, though softened by this device, represents the full depth of his fall into the sins of the flesh. It has been suggested by a colleague of mine that Wever is making a reference in this stanza to the doctrine of the real presence in the mass.
809. do not you passe] do not you mind.
811. proue] test.
821. hurly burly] tumult, uproar, confusion.
822. Smicke smacke] kissing; a jingling modification of smack.
823. ticke tacke] euphemism for sexual intercourse. See Shakespeare's use of this phrase in *Measure for Measure*, I. iii. 191-192.
827. smocke smell] bawdy sexual innuendo.
836. conceite] thought.
852. much fye vpon] an exclamation denoting disgust and reproach.
853. at twise] at twice: at two different times; at the second time.
867. sticke] hesitate.
869. and if] if.
898. lustes] desires.   swage] abate or soften.
909. His life is an abuse of, and insult to God's word.
911. conuersation] see note above, l. 236.
940. synnes and sice] pun on French *cinq* and *six;* fives and sixes, terms

GLOSSES

used in dice games.

947. Capernite] alludes to biblical story of Jews at Capernaum who were unable to distinguish between things of the flesh and the things of the spirit. John 6.63.

948. haddest leuer] had rather.

951. spyrt] spurt, an increased exertion for a short time.

954. trill the bones] shoot the dice. grote] groat, an English silver coin worth fourpence issued from the time of Edward I to Charles II.

961-963. Osey] Isaiah 3.8-9.

973. conuersacion] see note above, l. 236.

989. Galatians 5.16-24.

1001. iagge] to cut jags in or notch.

1006, 1008-1009. For him there remains no saving sacrifice, but rather a fearful judgment and hell fire.

1010-1012. Matthew 12.32.

1033. Wo worth] woe betide.

1058-1059. Galatians 5.16-24.

1077-1083. Luke 15.10-24.

1085-1087. Matthew 7.13-14.

1092. falshed] falsehood.

1100. ware] aware.

1131. squire] square.

1160. captayne] Henry VIII is referred to as "capten" in "a lytell treatyse in Englysshe called the Extirpacion of ignorancy," sig. [A.iii.ᵛ], part of colophon missing, printed by R. Pynson, n.d., but written during the reign of Henry VIII and dedicated to the Princess Mary.

Bibliography

Bale, John. *John Bale's King Johan.* Ed. Barry B. Adams. San Marino, Calif.: The Huntington Library, 1969.

———. *The Dramatic Writings of John Bale, Bishop of Ossory.* . . . Ed. John S. Farmer. 1907; rpt. New York: Barnes and Noble, 1966.

Bernard, Jules Eugene, Jr. *The Prosody of the Tudor Interlude.* New Haven: Yale Univ. Press, 1939.

Bevington, David. *From Mankind to Marlowe: Growth of Structure in the Popular Drama of Tudor England.* Cambridge, Mass: Harvard Univ. Press, 1962.

———. *Tudor Drama and Politics, A Critical Approach to Topical Meaning.* Cambridge, Mass.: Harvard Univ. Press, 1968.

Bolwell, Robert W. *The Life and Works of John Heywood.* New York: Columbia Univ. Press, 1921.

Bowers, Fredson. *On Editing Shakespeare and the Elizabethan Dramatists.* Philadelphia: Univ. of Pennsylvania Library, 1955.

Cowper, J. M., ed. *Four Supplications, 1529-1553 A.D.* EETS, ES, No. 13. London: for the Early English Text Society, 1871.

Cranmer, Thomas. *Certaine Sermons or Homilies Appointed to be Read in Churches in the Time of Queen Elizabeth.* Introd. Mary Ellen Rickey and Thomas B. Stroup. 1623; rpt. Gainesville, Fla.: Scholars Facsimiles & Reprints, 1968.

The Dramatic Writings of Richard Wever and Thomas Ingelend. Ed. John S. Farmer. 1905; rpt. New York: Barnes & Noble, 1966.

Duff, E. Gordon. *A Century of the English Book Trade* [1457-1557]. London: for the Bibliographical Society, 1905.

Duffield, Gervase E., ed. *The Work of Thomas Cranmer.* Introd., J. I. Packer. Philadelphia: Fortress, 1965.

A Dyalogue of Disputaciō bytwene a Gentylman and a Prest Concernyng the Supper of ẏ Lorde. n.d. STC 6800.

Elton, G. R. *Reform and Reformation: England, 1509-1558.* Cambridge, Mass.: Harvard Univ. Press, 1977.

The Enterlude of John Bon & Mast Person; A Dialogue, on the Festival of Corpus Christi, and on Transubstantiation. Ed. William Henry Black. London: for the Percy Society, 1852.

Erasmus, Desiderius. *The Colloquies of Erasmus.* Trans. Craig R. Thompson. Chicago and London: Univ. of Chicago Press, 1965.

Evans, G. B. "Shakespeare Restored — *Once Again!*" In *Editing Renaissance Dramatic Texts: English, Italian, and Spanish.* Ed. Anne Lancashire. New York and London: Garland, 1976, pp. 39-56.

Everyman. Ed. A. C. Cawley. Manchester, Eng.: Manchester Univ. Press, 1961.

Foxe, John. "Christus Triumphans." In *Two Latin Comedies by John Foxe the Martyrologist.* Ed. and trans. John Hazel Smith. Ithaca and London: Cornell Univ. Press, 1973, pp. 199-446.

Gayley, Charles Mills. *Representative English Comedies.* Vol. I. New York: Macmillan, 1912.

Gnapheus, Gulielmus. *Acolastvs, A Latin Play of the Sixteenth Century.* Ed. and trans. W. E. D. Atkinson. Univ. of Western Ontario Studies in Humanties, No. 3. London, Ontario, Canada: Univ. of Western Ontario, 1964.

Greg, W. W. *A Bibliography of the English Printed Drama to the Restoration.* Vol. I. London: for the Bibliographical Society, 1939.

―――, ed. *Shakespeare's Hand in the Play of Sir Thomas More: Papers by Alfred W. Pollard, W. W. Greg, E. Maunde Thompson, J. Dover Wilson, and R. W. Chambers*. Cambridge: Univ. Press, 1923.

Hawkins, Thomas, ed. *The Origin of the English Drama, illustrated in its various species, viz. Mystery, Morality, Tragedy, and Comedy, by specimens from our earliest writers*. Oxford: Clarendon, 1773. Vol. I.

Hazlitt, W. Carew, ed. *A Select Collection of Old English Plays*. 1874-76; rpt. New York: Benjamin Blom, 1964.

Henry VIII. *A Necessary Doctrine and Ervdition for Any Christen man, sette furthe by the kynges maiestie of Englande*. . . . London: Thomas Barthelet, 1543. STC 5168.

―――. [Another ed.] London: Iohn Mayler, 1543. STC 5175.

Heinze, R. W. *The Proclamations of the Tudor Kings*. Cambridge, London, and New York: Cambridge Univ. Press, 1976.

Heywood, John. *A mery play betwene the pardoner and the frere, the curate and neybour Pratte*. [London:] Wm. Rastell, 1533. STC 13299.

―――. *The playe called the foure PP*. London: W. Myddylton, n. d. STC 13300.

Heywood, Thomas. *The Dramatic Works of Thomas Heywood*. 1874; rpt. New York: Russell & Russell, 1964.

Houle, Peter J. *The English Morality and Related Drama: A Bibliographical Survey*. Hamden, Conn.: Shoe String Press, 1972.

Hughes, Philip. *The Reformation in England*. Vol. II. London: Hollis & Carter, 1953.

The institvtion of a Christen man, conteynynge the Exposytion or Interpretation of the commune Crede, of the seuen Sacramentes, of the .x. commandementes, and of the Pater noster, and the Aue Maria Iustyfication & Purgatory. London: Thomas Berthelet, 1537. STC 5163.

Kelly, Virginia Stuart. "*Lusty Juventus,* A Study in Lutheran Drama." M. A. Thesis Fordham University 1944.

Kolve, V. A. "*Everyman* and the Parable of the Talents." In *The Medieval Drama.* Ed. Sandro Sticca. Albany: State Univ. of New York Press, 1972, pp. 69-95.

Letters and Papers, Foreign and Domestic, of the Reign of Henry VIII. Preserved in the Public Record Office, The British Museum, and Elsewhere in England. Arranged and catalogued, James Gairdner and R. H. Brodie. Vols. XVI (1898); XVII (1900); XVIII, Pt. 1 (1901), Pt. 2 (1902); XIX, Pt. 1 (1903), Pt. 2 (1905); XX, Pt. 1 (1905), Pt. 2 (1907); XXI, Pt. 1 (1908), Pt. 2 (1910). London: for Her Majesty's Stationery Office.

Letters of the Kings of England. Ed. James Orchard Halliwell. London: Henry Colburn, 1848. Vol. I.

Locher, Gottfried W. "Zwingli and Erasmus." In *Erasmus in English.* A Newsletter pub. Univ. of Toronto Press, No. 10 (1979-80), 6-8.

Mackenzie, W. Roy. *The English Moralities from the Point of View of Allegory.* Harvard Studies in English, Vol. II. Boston and London: Ginn, 1914.

Matchett, William H. "Shylock, Iago, and *Sir Thomas More:* With Some Further Discussion of Shakespeare's Imagination." *PMLA,* 92 (1977), 217-230.

McKerrow, Ronald B. *Printers' & Publishers' Devices in England & Scotland 1485-1640.* London: for the Bibliographical Society, 1913.

Title-page Borders used in England & Scotland 1485-1640. London: for the Bibliographical Society, 1932.

Morrison, Paul G. *Index to Printers, Publishers and Booksellers in A. W. Pollard and G. R. Redgrave A Short-Title Catalogue.* . . . Charlottesville, Va.: Bibliographical Society of Virginia, 1950.

Nosworthy, J. M., ed. *Lusty Juventus.* Oxford: for the Malone Society, Univ. Press, 1971.

Pollard, A. F. *Henry VIII.* 1902; rpt. London and Harlow: Longmans, Green, 1968.

Thomas Cranmer and the English Reformation 1489-1556. 1905; rpt. New York and London: G. P. Putnam's Sons, 1906.

Punt, William. *A New Dialoge called the Endightment agaynste mother Messe.* London: Wyllyam Hyll and Wyllyam Seres, 1548. STC 20499.

Ribner, Irving. *Patterns in Shakespearian Tragedy.* London: Methuen, 1960.

Ridley, Jasper. *Thomas Cranmer.* Oxford: Clarendon, 1962.

Rossiter, A. P. *English Drama from Early Times to the Elizabethans: Its Background, Origins, and Development.* 1950; rpt. New York: Barnes & Noble, 1967.

Schoenbaum, Samuel. *Internal Evidence and Elizabethan Dramatic Authorship: An Essay in Literary History and Method.* Evanston: Northwestern Univ. Press, 1966.

——— *William Shakespeare: A Compact Documentary Life.* New York: Oxford Univ. Press, 1977.

Scragg, Leah. "Iago — Vice or Devil?" *Shakespeare Survey*, 21 (1968), 53-65.

Shakespeare, William. *A New Variorum Edition of Shakespeare*. Ed. Horace Howard Furness. 1886; rpt. New York: Dover, 1963.

Simpson, Richard. "Are There Any Extant MSS. in Shakespeare's Handwriting?" *Notes & Queries*, 4th S, 8 (1871), 1-3.

Sir Thomas More, A Play; Now First Printed. Ed. Rev. Alexander Dyce. London: for the Shakespeare Society, 1844. Rpt. in *Shakespeare Society of London Publication*. Vol. III. Nendeln, Liechtenstein: Kraus Reprint, 1966.

Southern, Richard. *The Staging of Plays Before Shakespeare*. London: Faber and Faber, 1973.

Spivack, Bernard. *Shakespeare and the Allegory of Evil*. New York: Columbia Univ. Press, 1958.

Strong, Roy. *Painting in England, 1540-1620: The Elizabethan Image*. New York: Arno, 1969.

Thomas, Helen S. "The Meaning of the Character Knowledge in *Everyman*." *Mississippi Quarterly*, 14 (1960-61), 3-13.

Turner, William. *A newe dialogue wherein is conteyned the Examinatiō of the messe*. [London:] John Day and William Seres, n.d. STC 24362.

The vpcheringe of the messe. London: John Daye and Willyam Seres, n.d. STC 17630.

Wager, W. *The Longer Thou Livest and Enough Is as Good as a Feast*. Ed. R. Mark Benbow. Regents Renaissance Drama Series. Lincoln: Univ. of Nebraska Press, 1967.

Wever, R. *An Enterlude called Lusty Iuuentus. Liuely describing the frailtie of youth: of nature, prone to vyce: by grace and good councell traynable to vertue.* London: Abraham Vele, n. d. STC 25148.

———. [Another ed.] London: Wyllyam Copland, n. d. STC 25149.5.

———. [Another ed.] London: Iohn Awdely, n. d. STC 25149.

Wilson, F. P. *The English Drama, 1485-1585.* Ed. G. K. Hunter. New York and Oxford: Oxford Univ. Press, 1969.